Blue Mountains
Best Bushwalks

2nd edition

by
Veechi Stuart

WOODSLANE

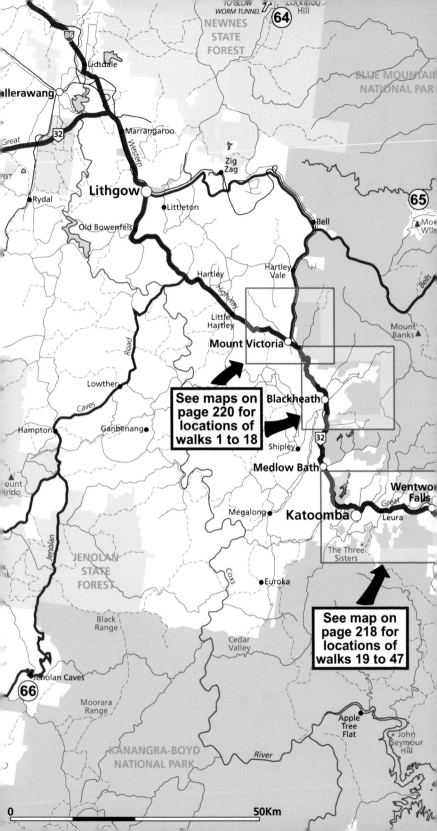

64

NEWNES
STATE
FOREST

TO GLOW
WORM TUNNEL

Lockatoo
Hill

BLUE MOUNTAIN
NATIONAL PAR

86

Lidsdale

llerawang

32

Marrangaroo

Zig
Zag

65

Great

Rydal

Lithgow

Littleton

Bell

Mo
Wil

Old Bowenfels

Hartley

Hartley
Vale

Mount
Banks

Little
Hartley

Bells

Mount Victoria

**See maps on
page 220 for
locations of
walks 1 to 18**

Lowther

Blackheath

Caves

Hampton

Ganbenang

32

Shipley

Medlow Bath

ount
indo

Megalong

Wentwo
Falls

Great

Katoomba

Leura

JENOLAN
STATE
FOREST

Coxs

Euroka

The Three
Sisters

**See map on
page 218 for
locations of
walks 19 to 47**

Black
Range

Cedar
Valley

Jenolan Caves

66

Moorara
Range

River

Apple
Tree
Flat

John
Seymour
Hill

KANANGRA-BOYD
NATIONAL PARK

0   50Km

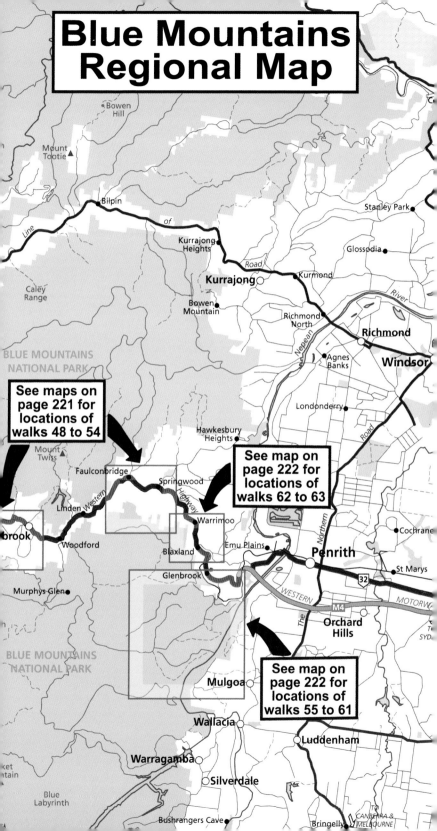

Woodslane Press Pty Ltd
10 Apollo Street
Warriewood NSW 2102
Australia
Email: info@woodslane.com.au
Tel: (02) 8445 2300   Fax: (02) 9970 5002   www.woodslane.com.au

First edition published in Australia in November 2006 by Woodslane Press
Reprinted 2007 (twice) and 2009.
This second edition published in Australia in November 2009 by Woodslane Press.
Reprinted 2011, 2012

National Library of Australia Cataloguing-in-Publication data

Stuart, Veechi

Blue Mountains best bushwalks : the full-colour
guide to over 60 fantastic walks / Veechi Stuart.
2nd ed.

ISBN 9781921606243 (pbk.)

Hiking—New South Wales--Blue Mountains Region--
Guidebooks.
Nature trails—New South Wales--Blue Mountains
Region—Guidebooks.
Blue Mountains (N.S.W. : Mountains)--Guidebooks.

Dewey Number: 919.440504

Printed in China by Bookbuilders
Front cover images: Three Sisters, Katoomba by Timapatt Talalak;
                    Greater Glider by Julian Robinson.

Blue Mountains
Best Bushwalks

2nd edition

Contents

Introduction

The Blue Mountains of NSW are an extraordinary environment for bushwalking. Even if you did a different bushwalk every day of every weekend for an entire year, you still wouldn't manage to explore every track. What you'll find in *Blue Mountains Best Bushwalks* is the cream of the crop, including short walks, half day walks, full day walks and an overnight expedition.

Walk grades and times

Every walk includes the grade, estimated time, total ascent, total descent and distance. Of course, estimating grades and times can be a little tricky. These grades and times probably err on the side of caution, but you'll soon figure out whether your own pace is faster or slower than what's shown in this book.

Easy: Suitable for all ages, but take care with children.

Medium: Some steps and stairs - for people who walk occasionally.

Hard: Steep stairs and steps - for people who walk regularly. Visitors with heart or breathing difficulties should not attempt these walks.

Very hard: Experienced walkers only. A high level of fitness and navigational skill required, minimum of three persons in the group. Advise friends or police of route and destination times.

Don't underestimate how much the total ascent or descent influences how hard you'll find a walk. A six-kilometre walk that's relatively level will take half the time of a six-kilometre walk that descends and then ascends 600 metres.

Introduction

Safety

Although many bushwalkers have died in the Blue Mountains, almost every one of these deaths could have been avoided using simple safety precautions:

Keep well back from cliff edges. Supervise children carefully and do not let them run ahead

Always carry drinking water. Sadly, you can't rely on the quality of any of the water in the Blue Mountains, especially after heavy rain. In summer, you'll need at least one litre per person for every two hours of walking (a frozen plastic bottle will ensure cold water for hours). In winter, you can probably make do with a bit less. A flask of hot drink is also a wise addition.

Keep an eye on the weather. Weather can change really fast in the mountains. If you're walking for more than a couple of hours, or if there are clouds in the sky, make sure you have wet weather gear as well as something warm. To check out the weather forecast, visit www.bluemountainsonline.com.au/weather.

Know your route and don't walk alone. Apart from the shortest of walks, you're best to walk with a companion, and on long walks, three people

Take care on wet rocks and steps

are better than two. Always make sure there's someone who knows where you're going and when to expect you back. Remember that on most walks in the Blue Mountains, you won't be able to get a mobile phone signal.

Wear sensible shoes. Choose your shoes carefully — no thongs or heels — and don't plan to break in a new pair of shoes just before heading off on a full day's walk. You're best to wear shoes that cover your feet and stay clear of long grass or thick vegetation.

Wear a hat and sunscreen. Regardless of the time of year, take sunscreen with you and wear a hat. In midsummer, be aware of the risk of heatstroke and if possible, try to walk early or late in the day. If you can't avoid walking in the middle of a hot day, avoid exposed ridges, cliff tops and fire trails.

Take some food with you. Hunger is a major cause of fatigue and if you're inexperienced (or walking with others who are inexperienced), food offers a chance to catch your breath and re-energise.

Carry a first-aid kit. A basic first-aid kit is a good idea. You're probably best to buy a wilderness first-aid kit off the shelf from an outdoors store, but if you decide to make up your own, it should contain adhesive strip dressings, antiseptic cream, a blister kit, an elasticised bandage, a foil rescue blanket, matches, sterile non-adhesive pads, painkilling tablets, a roll of sticking plaster, safety pins, scissors, two triangular bandages and tweezers. You may also want to take insect repellent.

Snakes

It is very unlikely you that will encounter a snake on any of these walks, as most snakes are more afraid of you than you are of them, and will only bite if trodden on, cornered or harassed. However, avoid striding through long grass, try to keep to tracks and if the path is obscured, make plenty of noise as you walk.

In the unlikely event that you're bitten by a snake, stay calm. Place a folded pad over the bite and then apply a firm bandage over the pad and as far up the limb towards the heart as you can. Remain as still as possible and keep the limb immobile using a splint if available. If the bite is anywhere other than your arms, do not walk but send somebody else for help or wait for a passer-by. Do not cut, suck or wash the bite and do not apply a tourniquet. Seek urgent medical attention. A description of the snake, and residual venom on your skin, will help with swift identification and treatment. Anti-venom is available for most snake bites.

Navigation

Navigation is one of the most important aspects of staying safe in the bush.

For harder walks, carry a topographic map and compass. Hopefully, the descriptions and maps in this book will help you find your way without a problem. However, some of the harder walks in this book describe tracks

Introduction

that are indistinct in places and for this reason, you're best to carry a topographic map of the area (1:25,000 scale) as well as a compass.

Consider purchasing a GPS. You can buy a handheld GPS unit for as little as $200, but be aware that you'll have to learn how to use it and in many areas of the Blue Mountains (particular in enclosed valleys, gorges or cliff ledges) the signal can be extremely poor or even non-existent.

Don't leave the main track. Even if you're concerned that you're no longer on the right track, don't leave a marked track and attempt to bush-bash to where you think the right track should be. Firstly, bush-

Signs can be very rare

bashing is usually painfully slow; secondly, you risk coming across sheer cliffs (either up or down) and thirdly, if you are lost, you're going to be much harder to spot if you've wandered off the marked track.

Up is home, down is away. Almost all the walks in this book start on the top of the ridge. For this reason, if you're at a track junction and you're in an absolute quandary about which direction to take (and you've already tried reading the map and the compass) then the rough rule of thumb is that 'up is home, down is further away'. Having said this, if you're seriously lost, you're best to stick near water and wait for help.

Call for help. Even if your mobile doesn't have enough signal strength to make a call, an SMS (text message) will often get through (although Triple zero doesn't accept text messages). Alternatively, if you have a GSM mobile phone, dialling 112 instead of Triple zero provides access to all networks, not just the network you suscribe to. Always give clear indications as to your location. The operator at Triple zero may be foolish enough to be asking you for the nearest cross street, but your message will be recorded so that rescuers can listen later, if need be. Tell them what you can see, the outline of the escarpment around you, where the sun is in the sky, if there's water nearby and whether you're on a ridge or in a valley.

Make yourself visible. If you know search parties are looking for you, make yourself visible from the air. If you have a bright coloured jacket or tent, spread it out in an open clearing or hang it from a tree.

If there's risk to life, activate a beacon (if you're carrying one, of course). A handheld EPIRB (Emergency Position Indicating Radio

Beacon) is a radio transmitter which, when activated, transmits an internationally recognised distress signal. EPIRBs are designed to be used when there is serious risk to life and when you have no other means of communication (such as mobile phone calls or flares). You can borrow an EPIRB for free from Katoomba or Springwood police station, and also from the National Parks office in Blackheath.

Track closures

All tracks in the Blue Mountains National Park are susceptible to closures with landslides, local flooding, bushfires and unsafe footpaths being just some of the causes. (Even at the time of writing, there are a couple of walks in this book temporarily closed for repairs.) For information regarding track closures or track conditions, phone the Blue Mountains Heritage Centre (T 4787 8877).

Looking after the bush

Chances are, if you're reading this book, you already know the basics. Take your rubbish with you, stay on the tracks, don't pick wildflowers, don't break branches off trees and don't blaze new trails. If there are no toilets, bury human waste at least 15 cm deep and at least 100 metres away from any water source. Leave your dog at home, and if you're lucky enough to see a wild animal, let it be (and don't feed it).

However, what you may not be so familiar with (especially if you come from overseas) is being responsible about possible fire. At certain times of year in the Blue Mountains, it only takes a single spark to create a fire that can get out of control and destroy thousands of hectares within a matter of hours, often threatening lives and property. For this reason, total fire bans are often in place between November and March and in extreme circumstances, some of the valley walks may even be closed.

You're best to check fire restrictions before setting off (**T 4782 2159** or **www.bluemountains.rfs.nsw.gov.au**). If there's a total fire ban, you won't even be able to use a camping stove and will have to take food that doesn't need cooking. If you're a smoker and there's a total fire ban, you'll have to either ditch your plans or leave your ciggies at home.

Walks at a glance

Water Access	Weather	Highlights
-	All conditions	Views, historic features
-	All conditions	Grotto, ferns, hidden cave
-	All conditions	Historic terraces, Bushranger's cave, mossy glens
-	Avoid hot summer sun	Wildflowers, hanging swamp, cultural features
-	Ideal in winter/spring	Historic tracks, views
Swimming	Avoid after heavy rain	Views, waterfalls, the challenge of a steep ascent
Swimming	Best when daylight is long	Views, camping, forest, wilderness
-	All conditions	Views
-	All conditions	Wheelchair & stroller access, views
-	All conditions	Wildflowers, views, Aboriginal cultural features
Paddling	Best in spring and autumn	Views, cliff top track
Paddling	Shadier in afternoon	Views, wildflowers, cliff top track
Paddling	Shadier in afternoon	Views, creeks, cliff top track
Swimming	Avoid during heavy rain	Creeks, canyon, rainforest
Paddling	All conditions	Wildflowers, views, waterfall, enclosed glen
Paddling	Best in spring and autumn	Creeks, birdlife, hanging swamp, views
Swimming	Avoid during heavy rain	Track cut into side of cliff, waterfall
Swimming	Best on clear, sunny day	Historic tracks, waterfalls, wilderness, rainforest
-	All conditions	Views, wheelchair/stroller access
-	Best in the moonlight	Night views, fairly silly but good fun
Paddling	All conditions	Hanging swamp, creekside walk, waterfall
-	All conditions	Views, cascades, visitor centre
-	All conditions	Views, café along the way, rainforest

Walks at a glance

Water Access	Weather	Highlights
-	Avoid windy weather	Views, café, cascades, rainforest
Swimming	All conditions	Views, historic steps, rainforest, ride back up the hill
-	Avoid in heavy rain	Canyon-like environment, waterfall
-	All conditions	Historic track, rainforest, fun rock scrambles (optional)
-	Best on a clear day	One of the best views in the mountains
Paddling	All conditions	Waterfalls, Aboriginal occupation shelter
-	Best on a clear day	Cascades, rainforest, views
-	All conditions	Wildflowers, views
-	Best on a clear day	Quiet sandy trail, wildflowers, exposed views
-	All conditions, even mist	Views, boardwalks, swamp
-	Best on clear, still days	Swamp, wildflowers, views, remoteness
Paddling	Ideal in warm weather	Rainforest, waterfalls, views
Paddling	Ideal in warm weather	Cascades, waterfalls, rainforest and a train ride up the hill!
-	Best on a clear day	Views
-	All conditions	Aboriginal cultural significance
Paddling	All conditions	Hanging swamp, waterholes
Paddling	Best on a clear day	Views, waterfall
Swimming	All conditions	Varied vegetation, views, secluded pools, cascades
-	All conditions, even mist	Views, cliff top track, varied vegetation
Paddling	All conditions	Hanging swamp, boardwalks, views, cliff top track
Swimming	All conditions, even mist	Historic track, waterfalls, views
Swimming	Ideal in warm weather	Waterfalls, Slacks Stairs, rainforest
Swimming	Ideal in warm weather	Challenging track, rainforest, waterfalls
Swimming	Ideal in warm weather	Waterfalls, historic tracks, solitude, rainforest

Walks at a glance

Walk title	Page	Grade	Time	Distance
Lawson to Springwood				
48 Picnics on Waterfall Circuit	154	Easy	1 hr 30 min	3 km circuit
49 Dreamy beauty of Terrace Falls	157	Easy	1 hr 30 min	2.8 km circuit
50 Martins Lookout to Lost World	160	Medium/Hard	3 hrs	6.3 km return
51 Bellbirds at Sassafras Gully	164	Medium	3 hrs	6.6 km one wa
52 Creek circuit on Wiggins Track	168	Medium	2 hrs 30 min	4.8 km circuit
53 Swimming holes on Glenbrook Creek	170	Medium/Hard	4 hrs	8.9 km one wa
54 Blue Gum Swamp	174	Medium/Hard	5 hours	9 km circuit
Warrimoo to Glenbrook				
55 Bird's-eye view from Nepean Lookout	180	Easy	40 min	1.4 km return
56 Kangaroos at Euroka	183	Easy	1 hr 30	3.2 km circuit
57 Rockhopping at Jellybean Pool	186	Medium	1 hr 30 min	2 km circuit
58 Yabbies and picnics at Crayfish Pool	188	Medium	1 hr 10 min	1.8 km return
59 Winter sun on Jack Evans Track	190	Medium	1 hr 30 min	2.5 km return
60 Rock art at Red Hands Cave	194	Easy	2 hrs	4 km circuit
61 Camp Fire Creek to Red Hands Cave	196	Medium	4 hrs	9.2 km circuit
62 Secrets of Florabella Pass	199	Medium/Hard	3 hrs 30 min	6.2 km circuit
63 Offtrack adventure along Glenbrook Creek	203	Hard	7 hrs	9.5 km one w
Exploring Further Afield				
64 Glowworms, canyons and railways	208	Medium	5 hrs	10.5 km circu
65 Canyons at Wollangambe	212	Hard	3 hrs	6.3 km return
66 Natural wonders of Jenolan Caves	215	Easy	1 hr	2 km circuit

Water Access	Weather	Highlights
Paddling	All conditions	Waterfalls, creeks
Paddling	Ideal in warm weather	Shallow pools, old tracks, rainforest, cascades
Swimming	Avoid hot summer sun	Views, challenging ascents, quiet track
Paddling	All conditions	Rainforest, birdlife, creeks
Paddling	All conditions	Rainforest, birdlife, creeks
Swimming	All conditions	Rainforest, camping, creek, waterfalls
-	Avoid hot summer sun	Birdlife, views, swamp
-	Avoid hot summer sun	Views, level track
Swimming	Ideal winter walk	Wildlife at Euroka, Nepean River
Swimming	All conditions	Rockhopping, wide waterholes
Swimming	All conditions	Quiet track, waterfall, beach
Swimming	Ideal in warm weather	Views, rockhopping, waterholes
Paddling	Ideal winter/early spring	Creekside track, aboriginal rock art
Paddling	Ideal winter/early spring	Creekside track, aboriginal rock art
Swimming	All conditions	Rock formations, birdlife, wildflowers
Swimming	Avoid hot summer sun	Off track, rockhopping, physical challenge
Paddling	All conditions	Historic features, glow worms, valley views
Swimming	Ideal in warm weather	Swimming, canyon environment, adventure
Paddling	All conditions	Caves, rock formations, creekside track

Mount Victoria

Elevation: 1043 metres   **Population:** 800

The most western village in the Blue Mountains, Mount Victoria retains a rural feel, with one general store that doubles as the Post Office, a cluster of antique stores, a couple of cafés, and some grand old buildings dating back to the late 1800s.

There's a strong sense of community in Mount Victoria. Unlike many of the other commuter-belt Mountain villages, it's a little too far to travel to the city everyday. Consequentially, the residents form an interesting mix of established locals, avid climbers and Sydney runaways.

Many of the local walks are full of history, with several tracks following the original roads that descended from the top of the Blue Mountains down to Hartley Valley. Other walks tend to be local secrets (tucked away on council land, rather than in the National Park) and although poorly signposted, are fascinating historic tracks in their own right.

PUBLIC TRANSPORT

Service 696 goes from Katoomba to Mount Victoria and back three times a day, on weekdays only. Within Mount Victoria, the buses don't venture far from the highway, meaning it's a fair hike to the beginning of any of the walks. (The closest is Walk 2, which starts 1.7 km from the railway station.) For most walks, you're best to rely on trains to get you to Mount Victoria, and from the station, use either the local taxi service (4782 1311) or a pushbike.

1 Looking out from Mt York

This short stroll takes you down a section of Cox's Road, the first road built over the Blue Mountains. This feat of engineering was built by 28 men in six months and ran 101.5 miles, all the way from Emu Ford to Bathurst. From the lookouts at the top, you look down to Hartley Valley and beyond to Jenolan Caves.

View looking north into the Hartley Valley

At a glance

Grade: Easy

Time: 30 minutes

Distance:
1 kilometre circuit

Weather:
Suitable for all conditions

Closest public transport:
Mount Victoria railway
station, 6.2 km away

Finding the track

From Mount Victoria railway station, head up to the highway and turn right. After one kilometre, Mt York Road turns off to your right. Follow Mt York Road right to the very end (another 4.8 kilometres).

Walk directions

1 At the end of Mt York Road, look for the sign saying Cox's Descent 1815 on the far right-hand corner of the turning circle.

2 Stick to the main track, ignoring the Alternative Descent track that branches off to your right. A minute after this, you see a commemorative plaque on a boulder. Bear right, following the original line of Cox's Road.

3 Only another 150 metres further on, you come to a track junction. Take the track back up the hill to your right, signposted as Cox's Alternative Descent.

4 You soon meet up with the main track again, but almost immediately turn right, following the sign that says 'To Lookouts'. Circle around past the lookouts (be careful with the first lookout as it's unfenced and rather exposed) until you arrive back at the Mt York parking area.

The track is fairly level and easy

Out and about — Mount Victoria

With its old buildings, country-style friendliness and art-deco antique stores, Mount Victoria can give you the feeling that you've stepped back in time. Another great way to sample an olde-time 1940's atmosphere is to pay a visit to the local cinema, Mount Vic Flicks. Consistent winner of the Best Country Independent Cinema award, the cinema screens Thursday through to Sunday (and daily during school and public holidays). With comfy seats, a well-stocked candy bar (where they serve you cups of tea in real china cups!) and a family vibe, Mount Vic Flicks (www.bluemts. com.au/mountvic, T 4787 1577) makes time travel seem almost possible.

2 Forest at Fairy Bower

This local favourite includes a secret grotto, a forgotten etching in the romantic 'Fairy Bower', a precarious ladder up to Cox's Cave and sheltered woodland gullies.

Finding the track

From Mount Victoria railway station, head up to the highway and turn left. Take the first street on your right (Hooper Street), turn left into Victoria Street (which soon becomes Carlisle Parade). At the T-junction, turn right into Mt Piddington Road and continue down the dirt until you arrive at a sign that says Mount Piddington. Steps lead up to a trig point and picnic area just behind this sign.

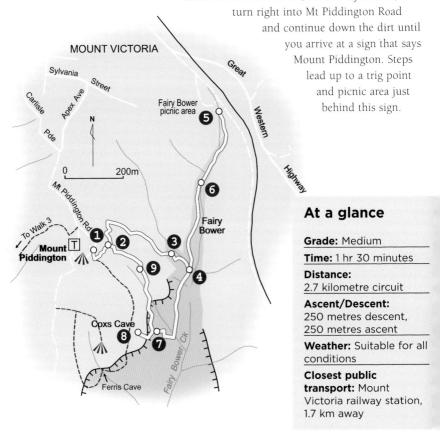

At a glance

Grade: Medium

Time: 1 hr 30 minutes

Distance:
2.7 kilometre circuit

Ascent/Descent:
250 metres descent,
250 metres ascent

Weather: Suitable for all conditions

Closest public transport: Mount Victoria railway station, 1.7 km away

Walk directions

1 From the picnic table, walk down to where the road loops around. On the opposite side of the road, you'll see a sign to Fairy Bower and Cox's Cave, with steps leading down. Head off on this track. After 50 metres, you come to a T-junction. Go left, following signs for Cox's Cave Circuit.

2 After a couple of minutes, you come to another T-junction. Turn left. From here, the vegetation thickens, with black wattles and hakeas forming archways overhead, and lyrebirds scratching and squawking underfoot.

3 Uneven stone steps descend to where a short sidetrack leads left to the 'Grotto', a cool but insect-ridden spot where a tiny trickle of water funnels down.

View from Mount Piddington

4 Continue your descent down mossy stairs till you come to another T-junction. Turn left over the wooden footbridge and follow the muddy creek up through the very pretty and rather romantically-named Fairy Bower.

5 After 15 minutes or so, you pop out at the Fairy Bower picnic area, next to the railway and the old tollhouse. Have a rest here, and then return back down Fairy Bower the way you came.

From inside Cox's Cave

6 On your return journey, about five minutes from the reserve, a small footbridge crosses to the right-hand side of the creek. Look to your right here, and you'll see the 'lady of the bower', a life-sized etching on a huge mossy boulder. Continue back to the footbridge where you turned left half an hour or so earlier (waymark 4 on the map). Go straight ahead now, as the muddy track meanders under sandstone overhangs. After 200 metres, the track emerges at an exposed outcrop and then curves around sharply to your right.

7 A short distance under a sandstone ledge takes you to the foot of a ladder. Up 20 rather precarious rungs (it's your decision whether you're up for this detour or not, but if you do, be really careful at the top), and then zigzag up a steep but short track to your left.

Ladder up to Cox's Cave

8 You arrive at the unsignposted Cox's Cave, a dome-shaped hollow where mineral salts streak white, ochre, green and black. From here, return to the base of the ladder and this time, turn left and head straight up.

9 You soon emerge onto the ridge. A rocky outcrop looks down into the tree-filled gully, where moulting bark lies thick on the ground. Continue up the hill, turning left at the track junction just below Mt Piddington Road. A few more zigzags and you're back at the road where you began.

Butterfly on grass tree flower

Track back up to Pulpit Rock

3 Bushrangers on the Zig Zag Track

At a glance

Grade: Medium

Time: 2 hours

Distance: 3.3 kilometres circuit

Ascent/Descent: 250 metres descent, 250 metres ascent

Weather: Suitable for all conditions

Closest public transport: Mount Victoria railway station, 1.5 km away

This beautiful old track features sweeping valley views, the romantic Bushrangers Cave, mossy glens and secret patches of rainforest. Take a torch so you can explore the hidden reaches of Bushrangers Cave.

Finding the track

From Mount Victoria railway station, head up to the highway and turn left. Take the first street on your right (Hooper Street). At the end of Hooper Street, turn right into Victoria Street then first left into Innes Road, which soon becomes Kanimbla Valley Road. The track begins at the turning circle where the bitumen ends.

Walk directions

1 Head down the fire trail for 30 metres or so and take the sidetrack that forks to the left. This sidetrack leads to the beautiful Pulpit Rock Lookout, with the Kanimbla Valley stretched out below.

2 Return to the fire trail and continue to the car park area. The Little Zig Zag track branches off on the left of the turning circle. Originally a bridle track down to the Kanimbla Valley, this track is a fine example of hand masonry, consisting of 17 stone terraces zigzagging from top to bottom.

Pulpit rock with the Kanimbla Valley below

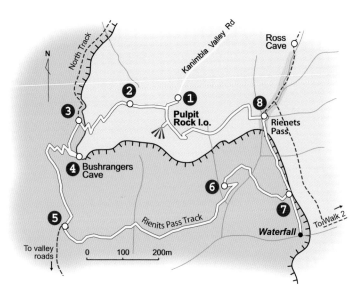

3 After about five minutes, the North Track branches off to your right (look for a blue-painted sign on a large boulder at the edge of the track), a favourite spot for climbers. Ignore this sidetrack and continue.

4 On the left, at the end of the 3rd 'zag' (the 7th turning), turn left at the sign that says 'Bushrangers Cave'. This sidetrack leads to Bushrangers Cave, a huge cavern that cuts 20 metres or so back into the cliff. Keen explorers armed with torches will be able to explore the narrow vertical passage at the back of this main cavern which opens into a secluded chamber. In 1897, a fragment of an old Sydney newspaper was found here, dated 1822, with government notices referring to the escape of four prisoners. Was this a bushranger hideout? After exploring the cave, return to the main track.

5 Wander down through the beautiful forest of banksias and Sydney peppermint trees till you get to the bottom of the zigzags. Head left, following signs to Rienits Pass, continuing your descent through dry open woodland. (Straight ahead, behind this sign, a leafy foot track descends to the Kanimbla Valley.) As the track levels, the vegetation changes and patches of black wattle, king ferns and sedges appear.

6 Look for wombat holes as you head north-east over mossy stone steps, traversing up the gully. You soon cross a narrow creek and views open up once more to the Kanimbla.

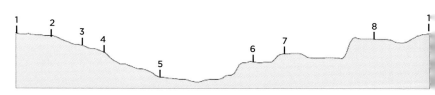

Views to Kanimbla Valley

7 You arrive at the base of the cliffs where signs indicate Ross Cave to the left, and 'Waterfall' to the right. Go right, and after a few minutes you arrive at a small waterfall, where a fine spray funnels through a narrow U-shaped cleft to the rocky pool below. Return back to the signs and this time continue straight ahead. The track soon starts to ascend up the left-hand side of a lovely ferny gully, known to locals as Wilsons Glen.

8 At a clear track junction, turn left following signs to Pulpit Rock, along a sandy ledge that hairpins sharply to the left. A short ascent winds up the hill for about 400 metres, leading past an unfenced lookout with distinctive red shale underfoot. You soon emerge at Pulpit Rock Lookout, where you started off.

Walk variations

From waypoint 8, instead of cutting back up to Pulpit Rock, you can go straight ahead, heading north following the watercourse. After five minutes or so, a sign points to Ross Cave on your left. After exploring the cave, continue straight up the hill until you come to a T-junction. If you turn left, the track pops out on Kanimbla Valley Road; if you turn right, you emerge on Carlisle Parade.

4 Solitude at Asgard Swamp

This walk is not one for spectacular views or breathtaking waterfalls. Rather it's a quiet, almost magical track through extraordinary bushland. For the original inhabitants, the wetlands of Asgard swamp would have provided a variety of food sources, and medicines including bandicoots, lizards, marsupial mice, snakes and swamp wallabies. This area contains a large concentration of Aboriginal cultural features.

At a glance

Grade: Medium

Time: 2 hours 30 minutes

Distance: 5.6 kilometres return

Ascent/Descent: 210 metres descent, 210 metres ascent

Weather: Avoid hot summer sun

Closest public transport: Mount Victoria railway station, 5.7 km away

Finding the track

From Mount Victoria railway station, head up to the highway and turn left. After 1 kilometre, just past the railway bridge, Victoria Falls Road goes off to your left. Proceed along Victoria Falls Road for 4.5 kilometres (it's a dirt road, but well-graded) until you see a locked gate on your left, next to a sign marked Asgard Swamp. The track starts at the locked gate.

Walk directions

1 Walk around the locked gate and follow the wide sandy fire trail (originally the old tramline leading to the oil shale mine) as it descends gradually through a forest of scribbly gum, black ash, hakea and tea-tree.

2 After a kilometre or so, you cross Asgard Brook, lined with sedges, swamp banksias and tea-trees. From here, tall scribbly gums line either side of the track, with creamy yellow trunks and silver-grey bark.

Asgard Swamp

3 Two kilometres from the start of the walk, look for an unsignposted sidetrack which leads left to a distinctive outcrop called Pagoda Rock, where you can enjoy fine views of Asgard Swamp below. At dusk, you may be lucky enough to spot swamp

Pagoda Rock

wallabies here. After some quiet time at this beautiful spot, return to the main fire trail and continue straight ahead.

4 After about 300 metres you come to a track junction. Head left. This section of track is narrow and rocky and descends relatively steeply. Through the trees, you can catch glimpses of the cliff walls on the opposite side of the Grose Valley.

5 You soon arrive at the historic oil shale mine that tunnels back under the base of the cliffs, and a little further on, the remains of a shale furnace with a gum tree growing out of it. The shale was mined in the late 1800s, an impressive venture considering the surrounding terrain. After exploring this area, return the way you came.

Old shale furnace

5 Historic mountain passes

This circuit starts from the end of Mt York Road and follows Cox's Descent, the first road over the Blue Mountains, built in 1815. You then return up the very pretty Lockyer's Pass, started in 1832 but never completed. For an outing that has a bit of everything, get an early start and treat yourself to lunch at the award-winning Collits' Inn (phone 6355 2072 for bookings). Work off any extra calories on the return journey up the hill.

At a glance

Grade: Medium/hard

Time: 4 hours

Distance: 9.5 kilometres circuit

Ascent/Descent: 260 metres descent, 260 metres ascent, plus 5 km of undulating track

Weather: Avoid hot summer sun

Closest public transport: Mt Victoria railway station, 6.2 km away

Finding the track

From Mount Victoria railway station, head up to the highway and turn right. After 1 kilometre, Mt York Road turns off to your right. Follow Mt York Road right to the very end (another 4.8 kilometres).

Walk directions

1 The end of Mt York road has a plethora of monuments, plaques, signs and memorials. You need to find the Cox's Descent 1815 sign that marks the beginning of the track on the far right-hand corner of the turning circle.

2 After about 140 metres, the track forks. Stick to your left, following the Cox's Descent 1815 sign. A minute or so further on, you arrive at a commemorative plaque, showing where the rock was cut with picks to let Governor Macquarie's carriage pass over the Blue Mountains in 1815. At this plaque, bear right (a sidetrack to your left leads down to a popular climbing area).

Original Cox's Descent

3 A short distance further on, you arrive at the site of the original rock-filled structure that bridged the gully. If you look carefully you can see hand-carved steps, drains and gutters. From here, tall, open forest leads down to the valley, following the route of early European settlers in their horse-drawn carriages.

4 At the foot of the descent, just past a huge termite mound, turn left following the Nature Track signs, skirting private property.

5 About 10 minutes further on, the track forks again. This time, leave Cox's Road and keep to your right, continuing due north along the fence line. The grazing land is beautiful here as you cross footbridges, balance along poles hammered into swampy ground and clamber over stiles. Soon the footpath becomes a 4WD track, winding gently northeast.

6 Look out for a sign on the right-hand side of the road that indicates the

start of Lockyer's Road, and head up this track. Sandstone edgings show where Lockyer began to build his road, a project that was abandoned in 1832, when General Mitchell shifted road gangs to his own road,

Victoria Pass (the current route of the Great Western Highway). The ascent is fairly gradual, leading up through boulders and at

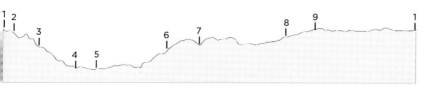

Rocky outcrops at the top of Lockyer's Pass

one point, beautiful old stone steps. This is a lovely quiet section of track, with varied woodland and abundant wildflowers

7 You soon arrive at a long rock formation

that marks the top of the ridge, with views down to the Hartley Valley and over towards Jenolan. An ideal resting spot. From here, you follow the top of the ridge. In spring, the yellow and brown flowers of dilwynia retorta (eggs and

bacon pea-bush) bloom either side of the track.

8 After a further 2 kilometres, the old coalmine track leads off to your right. Ignore this track and continue along the ridge.

9 Another kilometre or so and you arrive at a fork. Lockyer's Line passes through private land, so instead follow the Nature Track around to your left. After ten minutes or so you arrive at Mt York Road. Turn right. It's another 2.5 kilometres back to the end of Mt York Road, but a sheltered sidetrack runs parallel to the bitumen for most of the way. Interesting diversions en route include historic convict wells and the beautiful Barden Lookout.

Barden Lookout

Crossing the
Blue Mountains

When school children learn about Australian history, they learn that the names of Blaxland, Lawson and Wentworth are synonymous with 'opening up the interior', 'discovering that the only way across was to follow the ridges' and of course, being the 'first explorers to cross the Blue Mountains'. The ironic thing about this version of history is that it's largely false. It's true that in May 1813, Blaxland, Lawson and Wentworth (along with the emancipist Burns and three unnamed convict assistants, who probably did the bulk of the hard work) discovered that, by following the ridges, one could travel due west from Sydney across the mountains. It's true that they looked down from Mount York, and then from Mount Blaxland, and saw that the country to the west was more open and could potentially be used for agriculture. However, to say that the explorers 'crossed' the Blue Mountains is inaccurate. It was George Evans, six months later, who travelled four day's further west from Mount Blaxland to cross the Great Divide.

In his book *Blue Mountains Rediscovered* (published by Kangaroo Press in 1996), Chris Cunningham argues that there are several possible routes that 'cross' the Blue Mountains. The colourful John Wilson probably reached the Kanimbla via the Coxs River sometime between 1794 and 1796 and also pioneered the route of the existing Hume Highway to the open lands of Berrima in 1798. Francis Barrallier explored the route that leads to Mount Werong via the Wollondilly in 1802 and George Caley made it most of the way along the Bilpin Ridge in 1804. All of these discoveries were made well before 1813.

Why then is this glorified version of the discovery of the three explorers so persistent? There are probably many reasons, not least of which that up until that time, the supposedly impenetrable terrain of the Blue Mountains acted as a convenient prison wall that discouraged convicts from escaping. Added to this, the discoveries made by John Wilson, an ex-convict and outspoken free-thinker, were not given the same weight as those of the 'Macquarie Street boys', Blaxland, Lawson and Wentworth.

Of course, all of this focus on the European experience negates the fact that Aboriginal people had been travelling to and fro across the mountains for thousands of years. The Bell's Line of Road was an established trading route, as was the existing line of the Great Western Highway. The monuments at Mount York that celebrate the journey of the three explorers neither acknowledge this heritage, nor the fact that the building of a road across the mountains heralded yet more tragedy and dispossession for the Aboriginal population.

6 Swimming at Victoria Falls

Although the return journey from Victoria Falls is rather gruelling (a whopping 380 metres ascent), the waterfalls themselves are so beautiful that the trip is well worth it. There are actually two sets of falls close together — the Silver Cascades and then Victoria Falls proper. Depending on how much rain there's been, both make good spots for swimming.

Lower Victoria Falls

At a glance

Grade: Hard

Time:
2 hrs 30 minutes

Distance:
3.6 kilometres return

Ascent/Descent:
380 metres descent,
380 metres ascent

Weather: Suitable for all conditions, but be careful after heavy rain

Closest public transport:
Mt Victoria railway station,
6.7 km away

Walk directions

Follow the first three steps of Walk 7, up to where the track arrives at Victoria Falls. Return the way you came.

Eastern Water Dragon

7 Overnight in the Blue Gum Forest

Although the very fit could possibly do this walk in one day, the delights of the Victoria Falls, the Grose River and the Blue Gum Forest warrant making this a 2-day adventure, with an overnight camp. National Parks approve camping at Burra Korain or Acacia Flats only, neither of which are exactly halfway (Burra Korain is relatively close to the start of the walk; Acacia Flats relatively close to the end). But in summer, it's possible to walk down to Burra Korain at the end of a working day, camp overnight and then spend the next day walking to the Blue Gum and up Perry's Lookdown. (For more information about walking in the Grose Valley, see Walk 18.)

At a glance

Grade: Very Hard

Time: Best as a 2-day walk, at least 8 hours of continuous walking

Distance: 15 kilometres one way

Ascent/Descent: 630 metres descent, 630 metres ascent, plus 13 km of undulating track

Weather: Avoid in mid-winter when days are short and nights are very cold

Closest public transport: Neither the beginning nor the end of the walk is anywhere near public transport. You may be able to call a taxi from Perry's Lookdown using a mobile, but you'd need to research in advance whether you can get reception there. (Organising to leave a car at Perry's Lookdown, or to be picked up, is probably your best bet.)

Victoria Falls

Walk 7 Overnight in the Blue Gum Forest

Finding the track

From Mount Victoria railway station, head up to the highway and turn left. After 1 kilometre, just past the railway bridge, Victoria Falls Road goes off to your left. Proceed along Victoria Falls Road for 5.5 kilometres (it's a dirt road, but well-graded) until you get to the end of the road. Signs indicate where the track begins.

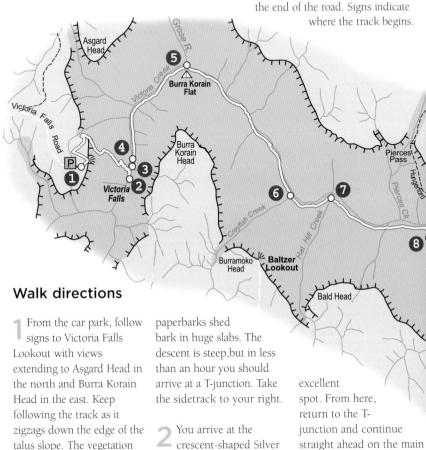

Walk directions

1 From the car park, follow signs to Victoria Falls Lookout with views extending to Asgard Head in the north and Burra Korain Head in the east. Keep following the track as it zigzags down the edge of the talus slope. The vegetation thickens, with tall tree ferns, black wattle, sasparilla and turpentines. Here and there, paperbarks shed bark in huge slabs. The descent is steep, but in less than an hour you should arrive at a T-junction. Take the sidetrack to your right.

2 You arrive at the crescent-shaped Silver Cascades, where the water tumbles down broad sandstone terraces into an oval pool below. An excellent spot. From here, return to the T-junction and continue straight ahead on the main track. Shortly afterwards, a sidetrack to your right leads to the top of Victoria Falls. Keep to the main track.

3 Just after passing along a narrow ledge, a short sidetrack leads to the base of Victoria Falls. These cavernous falls are awesome, with a large rock shelf that juts out like a table, and grey scree leading down to a shallow pool.

4 Just below Victoria Falls, the track crosses to the right-hand side of the creek. This crossing isn't signposted, but look carefully and you'll see a stone cairn balanced on a boulder and a white arrow painted on an adjacent rock. From here, the track continues down the right-hand bank of the creek. The track can be a little indistinct here and there, but usually only for a few metres as you scramble over a boulder or along a fallen tree. If you find yourself bush-bashing, return to where the track was clear and look again for the right way. If in doubt, stay close to the right-hand bank. About 1.5 kilometres after Victoria Falls, you arrive at a small camping area and fireplace by the edge of Victoria Creek.

5 Cross Victoria Creek and continue along the track for 50 metres or so until you arrive at Burra Korain, a flat grassy camping area that sits on the western junction of Victoria Creek and the Grose River. This is a beautiful spot at both sunset and sunrise when the sun hits the cliff walls and bounces off the water. After sleeping (or resting) at Burra Korain, the track rock-hops along the middle of the river for a few metres before resuming on the right-hand bank of the Grose, where the water runs broad and silvery.

N

0   1 Km

River

9

Little
Blue Gum

13 Perry's
Lookdown
T

12

Mount
Banks

10

Blue Gum
Forest
11

Acacia Flats

12 13

9   10   11

Walk 7 **Overnight in the Blue Gum Forest**

6 Shortly after you see the orange walls of Bald Head appear in the distance, you cross Crayfish Creek (2 kilometres from Burra Korain). Notice the huge (and very old) xanthorreas along the next section of track.

7 Another half kilometre or so and you descend a little zigzag to Hat Hill Creek. It's not safe to drink from any mountain creeks, but avoid this one in particular, as this is the creek into which Blackheath STP pumps its (treated) waste.

8 It's slow going from here for the next 1.5 kilometres, before you arrive at signs indicating where Pierces Pass (also called the Hungerford Track) forks off to your left, leading all the way up to Bells Line of Road. For thousands of years, the Aboriginal people used this pass to get up and down the escarpment. The area by the Grose River remains an excellent resting spot, with good swimming. Continue along the right-hand bank of the Grose, with Banks Wall towering high straight ahead.

9 Almost 2 kilometres beyond the Pierces Pass junction, you arrive at the Little Blue Gum forest,

Blue Gum forest

an open grassy area dotted with blue gums. From the Little Blue Gum forest, you cross several small gullies, sometimes climbing quite high along the right bank so that the Grose River is out of sight.

10 After about 45 minutes, you arrive at a sign saying Blue Gum Forest. You've arrived! The forest is extraordinary: stately tall trees with smooth white-blue-grey bark, reaching 50 metres or more overhead. Fires swept through the forest in November 2006, but thankfully the forest remains

relatively unscathed. Wander through and wonder.

11 After 700 metres or so, you arrive at a crossroads. Straight ahead (another few hundred metres) lies Acacia Flat camping area; to your left is the Lockley Pylon track, which leads first to the junction of Govetts Creek and the Grose and then way up to Mt Hay. You need to turn right, following signs to Perry's Lookdown. The climb out is a real slog, ascending over 600 metres step after step after step.

Clear pools in the Grose River

1957 bushfire memorial

Pink tongued lizard

if you're stuck in the valley during a fire, don't try to climb out.)

12 When things get really steep and you go up a gap between the cliff walls, you're about three-quarters of the way there. Shortly after that, you arrive at a plaque erected in memory of four boy scouts who died in 1957 while trying to climb out of the Grose during a bushfire. (The moral of the story —

13 One last short slog and you arrive at Docker's Lookout and from there, it's only a few minutes until you arrive at Perry's Lookdown car park.

For families — Climbing the walls

Mount Victoria attracts some of the best climbers in the world, and spending a couple of hours watching them do their stuff is a great way to amuse inquisitive kids. Popular climbing meccas include Mt York Road (there's a favourite spot just off Cox's Descent) and Mt Piddington (a track leads off to the right from below the lookout). If you have teenagers who are keen to have a go themselves, or maybe the adults are the ones who are feeling restless, lots of outdoor companies offer half or full-day rockclimbing and abseiling adventures. Two established and reputable local companies are Blue Mountains Adventure Company at www.bmac.com.au and High n Wild at www.high-n-wild.com.au

Grotto off Porters Pass

Blackheath

Elevation: 1065 metres   **Population:** 4,200

Not so long ago, Blackheath used to feel like the point in the Blue Mountains where Sydney suburbia truly finished and the bush began. These days, the proliferation of good coffee shops, gourmet takeaways and antique stores gives the town a bit of a different edge, but that old-fashioned atmosphere still exists underneath it all.

Perched at over 1,000 metres, Blackheath has a fairly cool climate and can be quite windy at times. However, the bush that surrounds the town has some of the best walks in the Blue Mountains, with cool canyons, pristine forests, waterfalls and cliff top views. If you're up for a long walk, then the Grose Valley is the spot to be (see Walks 13, 14 and 18); the Grose has a special magic all of its own, and is not to be missed.

PUBLIC TRANSPORT

With the exceptions of walks 15 and 16, most Blackheath walks are quite hard if you're travelling by public transport, as they start a few kilometres from the train station. Mobile phone reception is patchy at all three lookouts in Blackheath (Evans Lookout, Govetts Leap and Pulpit Rock), so test your phone before relying on calling a taxi at the end of your walk.

Local buses:
Route 698 goes right to the NPWS Heritage Centre near Govetts Leap, servicing the start of walks 9, 12, 13 and 18. This service goes along Evans Lookout as far as St Andrews Rd, stopping 2.5 kilometres short of Evans Lookout itself All bus services are infrequent on weekends, so check the timetables before setting out (www.bmbc.com.au, T 4751 1077).

Taxis: Phone 4782 1311 for the local taxi service.

8 Lonely lookouts at Pulpit Rock

Pulpit Rock offers three levels of lookouts, each one more exposed than the last, with views stretching to Mt Banks and Mt Hay in the east, and Evans Lookout and Govetts Leap in the south. The light is best, and the area at its quietest, early in the morning or late in the day.

There are three levels of lookouts at Pulpit Rock

At a glance

Grade: Easy (although there are lots of steps)

Time: 30 minutes

Distance: 850 metres return

Ascent/Descent: 65 metres descent, 65 metres ascent

Weather: All conditions, except thick mist

Closest public transport: Blackheath railway station, 5.5 km away

Finding the track

From the Great Western Highway, head down Hat Hill Road. The road turns to dirt after 3 kilometres and forks at the 5-kilometre mark. Take the right fork here, signposted to Pulpit Rock. The car park area is at the road's end, another kilometre further on.

New Holland Honeyeater

Walk directions

Steps down to the lowest lookout

1 The track heads down past a picnic table, shelter shed and toilets. Even though the lookouts are well fenced, the whole area is very precipitous, so keep an eye on young children.

2 After 300 metres, you arrive at the first lookout, where a detailed sign explains all the landmarks in the extraordinary 270° view. Despite the accepted terminology, the Blue Mountains aren't really mountains at all. In reality, the entire area is one huge plateau dissected by gorges and waterways.

3 Another 70 steps or so descend to the second lookout, reached by crossing a wooden footbridge with stomach-churning views on either side. The cliff walls here are incredibly sheer, but vegetation bursts out of every rock fracture, somehow eking out an existence.

4 The final lookout is even further down, perched right on the edge of the cliff. Look straight ahead to where Govetts Leap Falls plunges 180 metres down into the valley below.

5 Return the way you came.

For families — National Parks Discovery Program

Throughout the year, the National Parks and Wildlife Service run a series of walks, talks and tours called the Discovery program. Developed and led by a group of local rangers, the idea of this program is to share knowledge about the Blue Mountains environment and the history that created it.

Many of the Discovery activities are suitable for children and in the school holidays, there's usually a junior ranger program. For younger children, the spotlight walks held in the early evening are probably your best bet, as the pace is generally quite slow and tailored to whoever turns up on the night. The rangers take the group on what is usually a fairly short walk, using spotlights to uncover a hidden world of nocturnal wildlife.

The Discovery program in the Blue Mountains also employs Aboriginal guides to talk about the culture and traditional lands of their community. Spending time with these guides is an excellent way for children to start to understand the importance of our cultural heritage, and to appreciate the close connections between Aboriginal people and their traditional lands.

For more information, phone the NPWS Heritage Centre on 4787 8877.

9 Family fun on the Fairfax Track

This level bitumen track has been designed for all members of the community, providing full access for the disabled. The track winds down from the NPWS Heritage Centre, arriving at Govetts Leap Lookout. If you're on foot, a rough track runs alongside the road back up to the Centre, making for a shorter circuit. However, if you're pushing a stroller or you're in a wheelchair, you're best to return the way you came.

View to Mt Hay from George Phillips lookout

Finding the track

From Blackheath shops, head along Govetts Leap Road for 3 kilometres until you come to a small roundabout. Turn left into the NPWS Heritage Centre car park. The track starts at the far end of the car park.

At a glance

Grade: Easy

Time: 1 hour one way

Distance: 1.8 km one way, 3.6 km return, 2.2 km circuit (via road)

Weather: All conditions

Closest public transport: Bus 698 goes to the start of the walk (infrequent service only, check times)

Walk 9 **Family fun on the Fairfax Track**

Walk directions

1 Bear right at the sign marking the beginning of the Fairfax Track. You soon pass clusters of xanthorrhoeas (grass-trees) (Children may be tempted to break off the stalks when these plants are in flower (after all, these stalks have made excellent spears for many thousands of years!). This is a good time to explain why it's important not to damage the bush, and to explain how if left alone, the seeds will fall onto the ground and germinate to make new plants.

2 On a sharp bend on the track stands a mature Scribbly Gum, hollowed at the bottom. The scribbles (caused by the burrowing of insect larvae) are very distinct on these white barked eucalypts. From here, it's only a hundred metres or so before Geebung Grove (Geebung is the Aboriginal name given to the Persoonia species).

3 Wander on past Cone Stick Corner, Waratah Rest and Sunshine Bay. You'll often see Mountain Dragons along this stretch of track, one of the four species of dragon lizards found in the Blue Mountains.

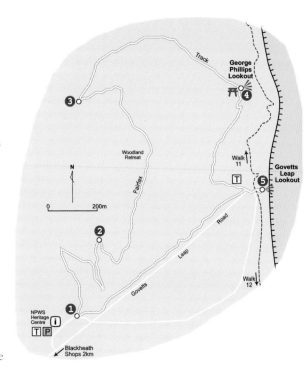

4 Before long, you emerge at George Philips lookout, complete with picnic benches and a shelter, where views extend all the way to Mount Hay and beyond. Be careful with children here; although the lookout is fenced, it's a long way down.

5 Now head through a hanging swamp area before emerging at the hustle and bustle of Govetts Leap lookout. The distinctive rounded peak almost due east is Mt Hay, over 9 kilometres away. From here, either return the way you came, or follow the rough foottrack that runs parellel to the road for 400 metres, back to the Heritage Centre.

The Fairfax Track is ideal for children.

10 Aboriginal heritage at Walls Cave

This short walk leads down through gardens of native wildflowers to where Greaves creek changed course many years ago, creating a small canyon where water cuts a tunnel through the rock. Just beyond this canyon lies Walls Cave, where Aboriginal activity dates back at least 12,000 years.

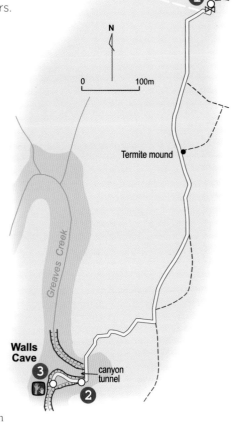

At a glance

Grade: Easy (although some steps)

Time: 1 hour 15 minutes

Distance:
1.4 km return

Ascent/Descent:
140 metres descent,
140 metres ascent

Weather: All conditions

Closest public transport:
Blackheath railway station, 4.2 km away (although an irregular bus service goes to Links Rd, 700 metres away)

Finding the track

From Blackheath railway station, head south along the Great Western Highway for 2 kilometres and then turn left into Evans Lookout Road. After 2 kilometres, turn right into Walls Cave Road. The track starts just beyond the Water Board gate at the end.

Walk directions

1 Go through the Water Board gate and follow the fire trail that descends diagonally straight ahead. Bush fire swept through this area in 2002, resulting in a riot of new growth along either side of the track, with a profusion of spring and summer flowering. Ignore the fire trails branching off to your left.

2 About 10 minutes from your starting point, you descend into a small gully, arriving at a bridge from which you can look right into a small tunnel-like canyon where Greaves creek runs dark and deep. This canyon was created when a landslide caused the creek to change course, many thousands of years ago.

3 Pick your way straight ahead over stepping stones for about 20 metres downstream along the creek itself to the path that leads from the right-hand bank. This path circles around to where a small viewing platform looks into the water-streaked amphitheatre of Walls Cave. This concert-hall shape has been created by the swirl of water as the creek rounds a sharp bend.

4 Return the way you came.

View into Walls Cave Canyon

Mountains history — Aboriginal heritage

The top 12 cm of archaeological excavation at Walls Cave showed that the terrace had been occupied since the creek changed course approximately 4,000 years ago. Further down in the dig, chert flakes and a buried hearth dated back at least 12,000 years. The real date of original occupation could be older still. It is likely that an extended family group lived in the area, at times moving between other significant areas in the locality such as The Rotunda (a large occupation shelter on the Grand Canyon track) and Beauchamp Falls (where an excellent source of chert was to be found, an ideal material for making tools). For more about archaeological excavations in the Blue Mountains, as well as fascinating accounts of Australia's Aboriginal heritage, get hold of a copy of *Blue Mountains Dreaming, The Aboriginal Heritage*, published 2009.

11 Cliff top track to Govetts Leap

This classic cliff top track starts at Pulpit Rock and then continues south-west along the escarpment, offering continuous views of the Grose Valley. A small detour along Pope's Glen makes for a quiet lunch spot shortly before the walk's end.

Finding the track

From the Great Western Highway, head down Hat Hill Road. The road turns to dirt after 3 kilometres and forks at the 5-kilometre mark. Take the right fork here, signposted to Pulpit Rock. The car park area is at the road's end, another kilometre further on.

At a glance

Grade: Easy

Time: 1 hour 45 minutes one way, 3 hours 30 minutes return

Distance: 4 kilometres one way, 8 kilometres return

Ascent/Descent: 175 metres descent, 125 metres ascent

Weather: Avoid midday sun in warm weather

Closest public transport: At the start of the walk, the closest transport is Blackheath railway station, 6 km away. At the end of the walk, Bus 698 runs from the NPWS Heritage Centre, 400 metres away

Walk directions

1 Head down 400 metres to the three levels of Pulpit Rock Lookout (see Walk 8 for more details). Enjoy the wild, precipitous views. From the lookout, head back up the footpath towards the car park.

2 About halfway between the lowest lookout and the car park, turn left, following signs to Govetts Leap. Different wildflowers bloom almost all year round along this first section of track.

3 Shortly after a rather bizarre picket-gate (complete with private sign) that appears in the middle of nowhere, you come to Boyd Lookout, from where you can see Govetts Leap, also known as Bridal Veil Falls. As the track winds along the cliff tops the vegetation changes a little, with damp gullies and hanging swamps. A little over an hour from the beginning of the track, the track descends into Pope's Glen. As you approach the creek, look for two distinctive Blue Mountain ash trees, striped like zebras.

4 Just after the creek crossing, the track forks. Turn right here, following signs to Pope's Glen.

Sunrise views

5 About 20 metres further on, a little beach makes a lovely paddling spot. Alternatively, keep going for about 150 metres until you arrive at Boyd's Beach. From here, return to the cliff top track and this time turn right, following signs to Govetts Leap.

6 A short ascent leads to a couple of lookouts: the first with views looking hard left to Horseshoe Falls; the second with good views of Pulpit Rock straight ahead.

7 A few more steps uphill and you arrive at Govetts Leap car park. From Govetts Leap, you can return the way you came. Alternatively, catch a bus or call a taxi back to Blackheath village (there's a bus stop and a public phone outside the NPWS Heritage Centre, just 400 metres along the road).

12 Govetts Leap to Evans Lookout

This windswept cliff top track leads through exposed heathland, swamps and gardens of wildflowers. If you're new to the Blue Mountains, then this walk is great for getting a sense of the land, with views extending all the way down the Grose Valley and across to Mt Banks and Mt Tomah.

Finding the track

From the Blackheath shops, follow Govetts Leap Road for 3 kilometres right to the very end. The track starts to the right of the main lookout and is signposted to Evans Lookout and Braeside Walk.

Walk directions

1 Enjoy the views at Govetts Leap Lookout, with Pulpit Rock on your left, the distinctive rounded cap of Mt Hay straight ahead to the east, and Govetts Leap waterfall tucked away to your right. Head right from the lookout, following signs to Braeside Walk. Descend steadily for 15 minutes or so.

At a glance

Grade: Easy/Medium

Time: 1 hour 15 minutes one way, 2 hours 30 minutes return

Distance: 6.2 kilometres return

Ascent/Descent:
150 metres descent,
130 metres ascent (one way)

Weather: In hot weather, avoid mid-morning and midday sun.

Closest public transport: At the start of the walk, Bus 698 runs as far as the Blue Mountains Heritage Centre, 400 metres away. At the end of the walk, the closest transport is St Andrews Rd, 2.5 kilometres away. Bus services are irregular.

Horsehoe Falls

Scribbly Gum

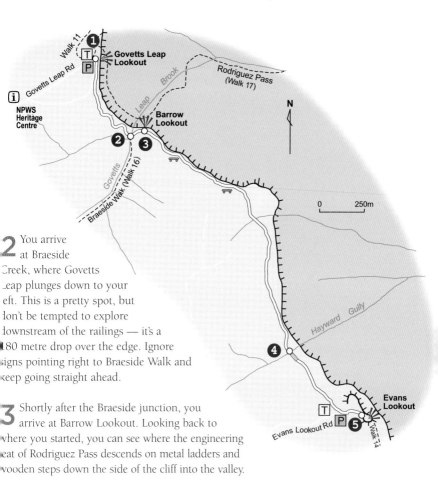

2 You arrive at Braeside Creek, where Govetts Leap plunges down to your left. This is a pretty spot, but don't be tempted to explore downstream of the railings — it's a 180 metre drop over the edge. Ignore signs pointing right to Braeside Walk and keep going straight ahead.

3 Shortly after the Braeside junction, you arrive at Barrow Lookout. Looking back to where you started, you can see where the engineering feat of Rodriguez Pass descends on metal ladders and wooden steps down the side of the cliff into the valley.

4 After another kilometre or so of undulating track, boardwalks cross the cool swamp of Hayward Gully. In hot weather, skinks and dragon lizards dart constantly across the track.

5 The track emerges at the car park at Evans Lookout. Turn to your left towards the noticeboards, and take the time to explore both of the lookouts here (Valley View Lookout and Evans Lookout) where the view over the Grose Valley extends all the way to the Blue Gum Forest. From here, either return the way you came, call for a taxi or head 2.5 kilometres down Evans Lookout Rd to where the elusive Bus 698 goes as far as St Andrews Rd. (If you can't get a signal on your mobile phone, try the public phone at Jemby Rinjah Lodge, 600 metres away on Evans Lookout Rd.)

View to Lockley Pylon

This cliff walk combines Walk 11 (which goes from Pulpit Rock to Govetts Leap) with Walk 12 (which goes from Govetts Leap to Evans Lookout).

At a glance

Grade: Medium

Time: 3 hours

Distance:
6.75 kilometres one way

Ascent/Descent:
315 metres descent,
255 metres ascent

Weather: In hot weather, avoid mid-morning and midday sun

Closest public transport:
At the start of the walk, the closest transport is Blackheath railway station, 6 km away. At the end of the walk, Bus 698 goes as far as Links Rd, 2.5 km away.

Finding the track

From the Great Western Highway, head down Hat Hill Road. The road turns to dirt after 3 kilometres and forks at the 5-kilometre mark. Take the right fork here, signposted to Pulpit Rock. The car park area is at the road's end, another kilometre further on.

Walk directions

The main thing to work out with this walk is the logistics, as you'll end up at Evans Lookout where there's no public transport and no public telephone (and predictably enough, unreliable mobile phone reception). Unless you're sure you can get mobile phone reception at Evans Lookout, meaning that you can call a taxi, this walk works best if you arrange in advance to leave a car (or a pushbike for each person) at Evans Lookout. If you get stuck, you can call a taxi from Jemby Rinjah Lodge, 600 metres away along Evans Lookout Rd. For more detailed walk directions and maps, see Walks 11 and 12.

14 The Grand Canyon circuit

One of the most popular walks in the Blue Mountains, the Grand Canyon is unusual in that it gives you a good sense of canyon scenery without the need for ropes and abseiling. Although much of the walk is along a edge that looks down from above, towards the end there's a dark, enclosed stretch along the floor of the canyon itself. Make sure to wear solid shoes with a good grip.

Finding the track

From Blackheath railway station, head south along the Great Western Highway for 2 kilometres and then turn left into Evans Lookout Road. Go along Evans Lookout Road for 2.9 kilometres until you see a car park area on your right.

At a glance

Grade: Medium (lots of steps, some slippery)

Time: 3 hours 30 minutes

Distance: 5.5 kilometre circuit

Ascent/Descent: 350 metres ascent, 350 metres descent

Weather: Ideal in summer but avoid during heavy rain and thunderstorms

Closest public transport: Blackheath railway station, 4.9 km away

Walk directions

1 A sign to Neates Glen indicates the start of the track. The track zigzags downwards, open woodland soon turning into damp forest. After 20 minutes or so, cross Greaves creek on a wooden footbridge and shortly afterwards cross back again. The vegetation is colourful and varied, with an abundance of waratahs in spring and flannel flowers in summer.

2 A short descent leads down to the 'Rotunda', a large overhang and Aboriginal occupation shelter. If you have time, take your shoes off and explore up the creek to your left, past small pools and hidden cascades. After exploring, keep following the creek downstream, following signs to Evans Lookout.

Storm gathering at Evans Lookout

Walk 14 The Grand Canyon circuit

3 You soon pass through a completely enclosed tunnel, created many years ago by a rock fall. Emerging on the other side, watch you don't slip as you pass under the spray of a waterfall. To your left, the chasm gets deeper and deeper. Just after the NPWS sign about safety in canyons, look for the gum tree perched on a natural bridge, with a huge drop below. This is one of the entry points where people abseil into the canyon itself.

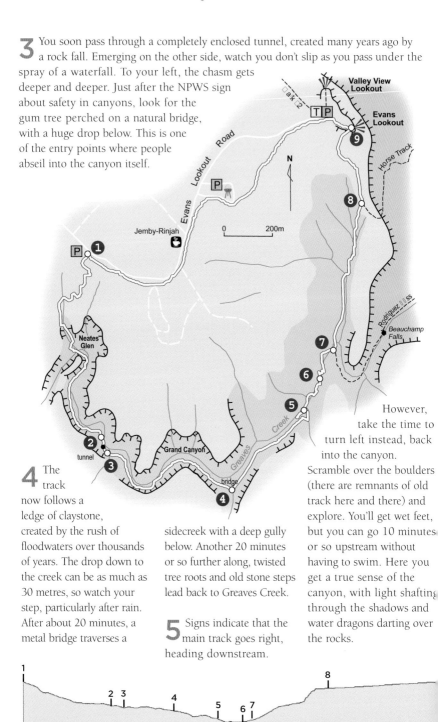

4 The track now follows a ledge of claystone, created by the rush of floodwaters over thousands of years. The drop down to the creek can be as much as 30 metres, so watch your step, particularly after rain. After about 20 minutes, a metal bridge traverses a sidecreek with a deep gully below. Another 20 minutes or so further along, twisted tree roots and old stone steps lead back to Greaves Creek.

5 Signs indicate that the main track goes right, heading downstream.

However, take the time to turn left instead, back into the canyon. Scramble over the boulders (there are remnants of old track here and there) and explore. You'll get wet feet, but you can go 10 minutes or so upstream without having to swim. Here you get a true sense of the canyon, with light shafting through the shadows and water dragons darting over the rocks.

6 Returning to the main track, follow signs to Evans Lookout. You soon find yourself picking your way over stepping stones along the floor of the canyon. It's tranquil and sheltered here; surprisingly cool even on the hottest of days. At the end of this stretch, a footbridge crosses a pool. A couple of minutes further on you arrive at a junction.

7 Straight ahead leads to Beauchamp Falls and Junction Rock. Head up to your left however, leaving Greaves Creek and following signs to Evans Lookout. The ascent is steep, but easy to follow.

8 A narrow saddle to your right marks the beginning of the Horse Track, an alternative route to the Grose Valley (see page 63 for details). Ignore this sidetrack and continue your ascent.

The floor of the Grand Canyon

9 You'll arrive at Evans Lookout. To return to Neates Glen carpark, follow the footpath that runs parallel to Evans Lookout Road for 1.5 kilometres.

Mountains environment — Canyons

Geologists think that canyons are formed by water running down planes of weakness in the rock. Looking around the Grand Canyon you can see at a glance how the power of water has eroded and shaped the rock formations, creating a deep slot up to 30 metres deep and only a few metres wide. Many of the undercuts and deep furrows in the rock walls have been formed by flowing water. When the creek flows fast, sometimes flash-flooding, sediments and small stones are carried along by the rushing water and cut against the canyon walls, acting as an abrasive. In this part of the Blue Mountains, canyons only form in a soft layer of rock called Burra-Moko sandstone.

15 Mystery tour of Porters Pass

Hidden away on the western side of Blackheath, Porters Pass is one of the oldest tracks in the Blue Mountains, dating back to 1888. This mystery tour takes you along the precipitous Walls Ledge, down the side of a waterfall and across Colliers Causeway. You then zigzag up Porters Pass, cut across escarpment heathland and complete your circuit through the dark and mossy Centennial Glen.

At a glance

Grade: Medium

Time: 2 hours 45 minutes

Distance:
5.5 kilometres circuit

Ascent/Descent:
215 metres descent,
215 metres ascent

Weather: Suitable for all conditions

Closest Public Transport:
Blackheath railway station,
1.8 km away

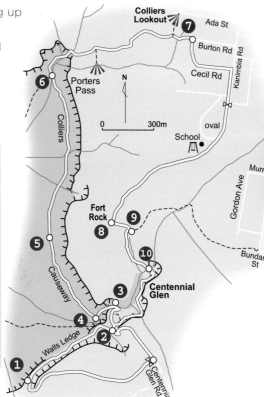

Finding the track

Cross the railway tracks at Blackheath, heading south along Station Street and then right into Shipley Road. After 800 metres, turn right into Centennial Glen Road. The track starts on the firetrail that leads off to your left at the end of this road, behind a locked gate.

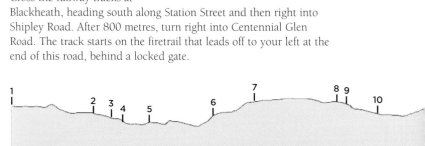

Walk directions

1 Follow the firetrail as it becomes a narrow track, dropping down into a gully and doubling back under a long claystone ledge known as Walls Ledge.

2 Past a shady gully, you arrive at the first track junction. To your right, a track goes back up to where you started. Keep going straight ahead, keeping your eyes open for another track junction (unsignposted) about 30 metres further on. At this point, follow the steps leading down to your left.

3 You soon arrive at a ledge by the creek's edge. Take the time to explore the shadowy grotto on your right, where a waterfall funnels down to a dark pool below.

4 More steep steps lead down the side of an exposed waterfall. Go slowly here and keep a hold of the handrail. At the bottom of the falls, you need to cross the creek. Things get a little indistinct here, but once past the big boulder in the middle of the creek, the track picks up again.

5 You're now on Colliers Causeway, with overhanging cliffs on your right and Kanimbla valley opening out on your left.

Steps leading down the waterfall

Walk 15 **Mystery tour of Porters Pass**

Dark steps down to Centennial Glen.

exposed heathland here turns into a carpet of flowering kunzea in spring.

8 After about 10 minutes, you arrive at a rocky outcrop known as Fort Rock. A sidetrack detours to your right (due west) to the cliff edge, but instead keep going, winding down to a rock platform.

9 At the rock platform, head right, following signs to Centennial Glen. Follow steps carved into the rock and descend down to your right, back into the gully. At first, the track is narrow and eroded, but soon arrives at damp, mossy steps that descend through a gap in the cliff line.

10 You're now at Centennial Glen (a favourite spot with climbers), where the track follows a narrow ledge under the cliffs, ducking under a waterfall at one point. A track junction indicates Porters Pass going down to your right. Keep going straight ahead, until you come to the signpost you saw near the beginning of your walk (waypoint 2). Head up to your left, following steps that lead back up to Centennial Road.

Look for forked sundew on the mossy rocks, as well as blue sun-orchids and purple milkwort underfoot.

6 After about a kilometre, cross a stream and climb the mossy, uneaven steps of Porters Pass itself, through black wattles, ferns and possum woods.

7 You'll emerge at Burton Street. Take the firetrail immediately on your right, and then turn left into Cecil Rd and right into Kanimbla Rd. At the end of Kanimbla Rd, pick up the firetrail that skirts the left-hand side of Gateway Christian School, heading south along the top of the escarpment. The

Walk variation

If you're travelling with public transport, take the sidetrack that leads due east from waypoint 9. This track emerges at Bundarra Street and from there, it's only 350 metres back to Blackheath station.

Scribbly gum

Trigger plant

Mountain Devil

Gum leaf

Mountains environment — The seasons

Many Europeans find it difficult to perceive the seasons in the Australian bush. After all, when you're used to spring blossoms, summer greens, autumn browns and winter greys, the bush really does seem evergreen. But look a little closer, and you realise that although Australian eucalypts don't lose their leaves every autumn, most do shed their bark. The old bark peels off in strips often several metres long, exposing contrasting new bark underneath and creating colourful patterns of reds, silvers, browns and whites.

The other special thing about Australian seasons is the way there is always something flowering — even in mid-winter, whole stretches of tracks are lined with flowering acacias and many other flowering species.

This grand circuit wanders down Popes Glen creek from Blackheath village all the way to the escarpment, follows the cliff tops along to the top of Bridal Veil Falls, and then loops back along Braeside Creek to where you started. This walk is great if you're relying on public transport as it starts and finishes relatively close to Blackheath train station.

Finding the track

Go down Govetts Leap Road (where the shops are) and take the third street on your left (Prince Edward Street). Go to the end and turn right into Wills Street. After about 200 metres, Wills Street becomes Dell Street and almost immediately after this you'll see a large purple sign on the right-hand side of the road, indicating the track to Popes Glen.

Walk directions

1 A narrow path leads behind the houses, running parallel to the creekline.

2 The track crosses Popes Glen Creek on a wooden footbridge. Continue alongside the creek for another kilometre (ignore old fire trails leading off to the right and the left). There's a thick mix of ferns and sedges underfoot with a forest of Blue Mountains Ash on either side. On misty days, these trees shine so white they seem almost ghost-like.

At a glance

Grade: Medium

Time: 4 hours

Distance:
7.8 kilometres circuit

Ascent/Descent:
250 metres descent,
250 metres ascent

Weather: Best in spring or autumn

Closest public transport:
Blackheath railway station, 1.5 km away

Popes Glen Creek

3 After you cross the creek, continue on the left-hand side for 400 metres and then cross back.

4 You will arrive at a track junction. If you like, check out Boyds Beach, a short diversion to a sandy area with a shallow paddling pool. Otherwise, turn to your right, following signs to Govetts Leap. A few metres further on, there's another sheltered beach with a slightly deeper swimming hole.

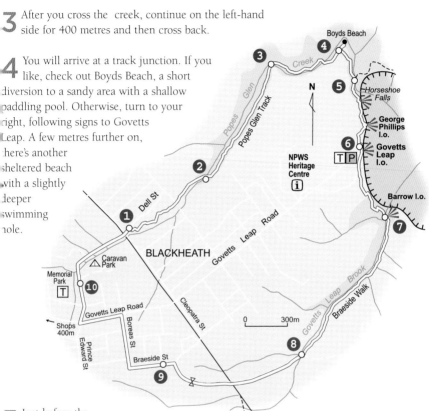

5 Just before the escarpment opens up, the track forks. To your left, the track crosses the creek and heads towards Pulpit Rock. However you will need to keep to your right, still following signs to Govetts Leap.

6 The track ascends now, past lookouts with views looking hard left to Horseshoe Falls, where Popes Glen Creek tumbles down. A little further uphill and you arrive at Govetts Leap car park.

7 From the car park, keep going straight ahead along the cliff tops, following signs to Evans Lookout. The track descends steadily for 15 minutes or so until arriving at Govetts Leap Brook. Just to your left, Govetts Leap plunges 180 metres over the cliff edge (don't be tempted to explore downstream here, the rocks are very slippery). Cross the creek and turn right, following signs to Braeside Walk.

Walk 16 Birdlife at Popes Glen

Walk variations

This walk connects with many other tracks along the way, making for lots of different walk combinations. at waypoint 5, the cliff top track continues north to Pulpit Rock (walk 11) and at waypoint 7, the cliff top track heads south-east to Evans Lookout (walk 12). At waypoint 6, Rodriguez Pass leads down to Govetts Leap Falls and the Grose Valley (walks 17 and 18). Just south of waypoint 8, a firetrail cuts southwest to Evans Lookout Road, emerging just north of the Grand Canyon Track (walk 14). Alternatively, a delightful short walk option is simply to walk the Popes Glen Track between waypoints 1 and 5, returning the way you came.

8 Although this track can be a little rough and wet in places, it's very picturesque, leading through gardens of flowering shrubs, dotted with scribbly gums. After about half an hour you arrive at the old railway water supply dam. Here you cross the creek one last time and ascend up to the fire trail on the other side.

9 Follow the fire trail till it joins Braeside Street. Turn left, then third right into Boreas Street, third left into Govetts Leap Road, and then second right into Prince Edward Street.

The top of Govetts Leap

10 You pass the Memorial Park on your left (with great swimming in summer) and the Caravan Park on your right. From here, loop around into Wills Street and then Dell Street, back to where the walk began at Popes Glen.

Mountains environment — Termite mounds

When you're walking, look out for termite mounds, the huge rounded piles of dirt up to 2 metres high. Termite mounds are amazing feats of insect engineering, where termites mix together with mud and saliva to form a cement-like substance. A single mound can take over 50 years to complete (although many mounds are older than this) and can contain several million termites, as well as multiple chambers. The bulk of the nest is actually underground, where a network of tunnels forms an air-conditioning system that's up to 10 metres deep.

17 Cliff descent down Rodriguez Pass

At a glance

Grade: Medium/Hard (not suitable for young children)

Time: 1 hour 30 minutes

Distance: 1.5 kilometres return

Ascent/Descent: 250m descent, 250m ascent

Weather: Avoid in heavy rain

Closest public transport: Bus 698 runs as far as the NPWS Heritage Centre, 400 metres away

To descend Rodriguez Pass is to marvel at the tenacity and imagination of Tomas Rodriguez, the local stationmaster who surveyed the route in 1898, making a reality of what others had considered quite impossible. 905 steps lead down an almost vertical descent to the foot of Bridal Veil Falls.

Finding the track

From the Blackheath shops, follow Govetts Leap Road for 3 kilometres right to the very end. To the left of the main lookout, steps lead down to an information board and behind this board, a track leads down to your right, with a sign saying 'Grose Valley Walks'.

At the foot of Bridal Veil Falls

Walk 17 **Cliff descent down Rodriguez Pass**

Walk directions

1 The track starts to descend almost immediately. Ignore the Loop Track going off to your left after 130 metres. Two lookouts offer clear views of Govetts Leap to your right (the very bottom of these falls is where you're heading).

2 After 250 metres of steep descent, you arrive at the base of Govetts Leap, formerly known as Bridal Veil Falls ('leap' is a Scottish word meaning 'waterfall'). These falls look different every time you visit, as varying wind conditions catch the spray of the falls in the changing light of each day.

3 After exploring around and below the falls a little, return the way you came (just don't look down!)

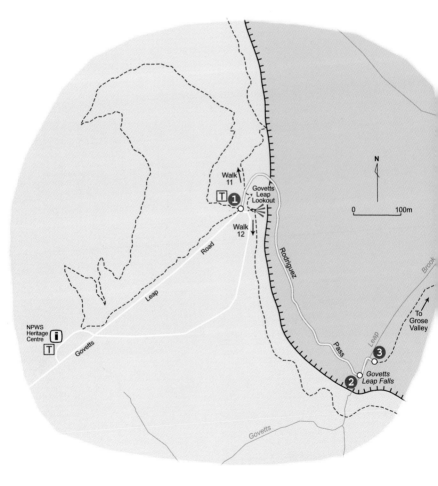

The engineering feat of Rodriguez Pass

For families — Walking safely along the cliff tops

Although the cliff walks around Blackheath are in many ways quite suitable for children (they're relatively level, quite short and there's lots to see), there's often a sheer drop of some 200 metres on the exposed side of the track. Even though most of the lookouts are fenced, large stretches of track between lookouts are entirely unfenced. Keep an eye on your children at all times and above all, don't let them run ahead out of sight. The cliff top track from Govetts Leap to Evans Lookout (see Walk 12) is less exposed than the track from Pulpit Rock to Govetts Leap (Walk 11).

18 Exploring the Grose Valley

The Grose Valley is one of the most special places in all of the Blue Mountains. The steep escarpment walls that enclose the valley on all sides create an environment where only walkers go, where there are no fire trails, power lines or roads, and where the calls of birds and frogs and the running of water are the only sounds to be heard.

Track Details

There are seven different generally recognised tracks leading into the Grose Valley, numbered on the map overleaf.

1 **Victoria Falls to Burra Korain.** This track starts from the end of Victoria Falls Road in Mount Victoria. (For more detail, see Walk 7.) The distance from the top of the track to the Upper Grose is 2.75 km, with a steep descent of 400 metres. The closest public transport is Mount Victoria railway station, 6.5 km away.

At a glance

Grade: Very Hard

Time: 1 to 2 days

Distance:
From 6 to 22 km

Ascent/Descent: Minimum 500 metres descent, 500 metres ascent

Weather: Best on clear, sunny days

Closest public transport: See individual track descriptions for details

Walk 18 **Exploring the Grose Valley**

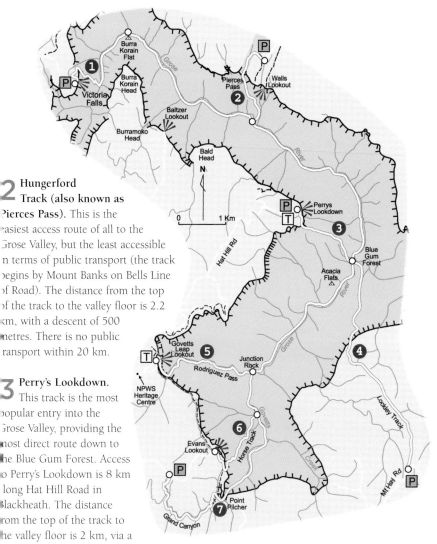

2 **Hungerford Track (also known as Pierces Pass).** This is the easiest access route of all to the Grose Valley, but the least accessible in terms of public transport (the track begins by Mount Banks on Bells Line of Road). The distance from the top of the track to the valley floor is 2.2 km, with a descent of 500 metres. There is no public transport within 20 km.

3 **Perry's Lookdown.** This track is the most popular entry into the Grose Valley, providing the most direct route down to the Blue Gum Forest. Access to Perry's Lookdown is 8 km along Hat Hill Road in Blackheath. The distance from the top of the track to the valley floor is 2 km, via a steep track with hundreds of steps descending over 600 metres. The closest public transport is Blackheath Railway Station, 8 km away.

4 **Lockley Pylon via Mount Hay.** This track leads off Mount Hay Road and goes via the cone-shaped Lockley Pylon (see Walk 34 for details). The section of track below Du Faur Head is a little rough, and is arguably easier to go down than to go up. The distance from the top of the track to the valley floor is 5.6 km, with a descent of 580 metres. The closest public transport is Leura Railway Station, 11 km away.

5 **Rodriguez Pass (Govetts Leap section).** Surveyed by the local stationmaster Tomas Rodriguez in 1898, this seemingly impossible route involves over 900 steps, making an almost vertical descent to the foot of Govetts Leap (see Walk 17 for details of the initial descent). The distance from the top of the track to the valley floor is 3 km, with a descent of 620 metres. The

Grose Valley rainforest

Edenderry Falls

losest public transport is
Blackheath Railway Station,
5.2 km away (although
infrequent buses go to
NPWS centre, 500 metres
away).

6 The Horse Track.
Originally an old bridle
track, the Horse Track is no
longer maintained by
National Parks and is
currently in poor condition
(contact NPWS on 4787
8877 for details). You access
this track from Evans
Lookout Road, taking an
unsignposted spur to your
left 450 metres from the
beginning of the Grand
Canyon Track. The distance

from the top of the track to
the valley floor is 2.3 km—
a slippery zigzag descent of
600 metres. The closest
public transport is
Blackheath Railway Station,
6 km away (although
infrequent buses go within
3 km).

**7 Grand Canyon,
Beauchamp Falls,
Govetts Creek.** At the time
of writing, this track is
closed due to a landslide
near Beauchamp Falls, so
check with NPWS before
considering this route. This
track is accessed from the
Neates Glen car park on
Evans Lookout Road (see

Walk 14 for details). The
distance from the top of the
track to the valley floor is
5.0 km, with a descent of
630 metres. The canyon
environment, pristine
beauty of Beauchamp Falls
and old stone steps leading
through thick forest make
this one of the most
spectacular access routes.
The closest public transport
is Blackheath Railway
Station, 4.6 km away
(although infrequent buses
go within 1.3 km).

Walk 18 Exploring the Grose Valley

Distances

The distance table below gives you an idea of the distances between the various entry and exit points to the Grose Valley. When planning your trip, don't overestimate what you or your group are capable of. All routes into the Grose involve both a descent and an ascent of at least 500 metres. Many of the routes are rough going with tracks that are slippery, overgrown, steep, or all three.

Unless you're already familiar with the Grose, you're best to allow a night's overnight camping at Burra Korain or Acacia Flats for any routes that exceed 10 kilometres.

	Vic Falls Rd	Burra K	Base of HP	Top of Hford	Blue Gum	Top of Perrys	Acacia Flats	Mount Hay Road	Govetts Leap	Junction Rock	Base of Horse
Burra Korain	2.8										
Base of Hungerford	6.7	3.9									
Top of Hungerford	8.9	6.1	2.2								
Blue Gum Forest	11.5	8.7	4.8	7.0							
Top of Perrys	13.7	10.9	7.0	9.2	2.2						
Acacia Flats	12.1	9.3	5.4	7.6	0.6	2.8					
Mount Hay Road	17.0	14.2	10.3	12.5	5.5	7.7	6.1				
Govetts Leap	18.3	15.5	11.6	13.8	6.8	9.0	6.2	12.3			
Junction Rock	15.3	12.5	8.6	10.8	3.8	6.0	3.2	9.3	3.0		
Base of Horse Track	16.3	13.5	9.6	11.8	4.8	7.0	4.2	10.3	4.0	1.0	
Neates Glen	21.8	19.0	15.1	17.3	10.3	12.5	9.7	15.8	9.5	6.5	5.5

Camping

National Parks only approve camping at Burra Korain (2.8 km from the head of the Victoria Falls track) or Acacia Flats (600 metres from the Blue Gum Forest). You don't need to book or pay for camping, but facilities are limited. Acacia Flats has 30 camping sites and compost toilets. Burra Korain only has a couple of camping areas, and has no toilet facilities. At both sites, you need to bring a fuel stove for cooking (open fires aren't permitted) and it's advisable to boil all water before drinking.

The other alternative is to camp at Perry's Lookdown car park, perched by a panoramic lookout with immediate access to the Perry's Lookdown track. Perry's Lookdown has 5 sites and compost toilets. There's no water available, and you need to bring a fuel stove.

Camping at Acacia Flats

Walking along Govetts Creek

Access

If you have a car and you're happy to enter and exit the Grose Valley on the same route, then access to the Grose is easy. The quickest way down to the Blue Gum Forest (one of the highlights of the Grose Valley) is via Perry's Lookdown, and a trip down to the Blue Gum via this route is a straightforward day's walk.

The logistical challenge comes if you decide you want to exit via a different route, as the only access that's close to public transport is Rodriguez Pass (by Govetts Leap in Blackheath). Possible routes are to take a taxi to the top of Victoria Falls, Perrys Lookdown, Neates Glen, Lockley Pylon or Evans Lookout, and then exit via Rodriguez Pass. Don't rely on getting mobile phone reception in order to call a taxi from any of these access points, as reception can be patchy with many of the networks.

With any route that involves a circuit, phone NPWS first on 4787 8877 and check for track closures (track closures are relatively frequent, due to fires, landslides and track maintenance).

Safety

The Grose Valley is a wilderness area, so remember to read the safety information at the front of this book before setting out. Both Katoomba Police Station and the NPWS Heritage Centre in Blackheath lend EPIRBs (emergency beacons) to walkers.

Out and about — Discovering Blackheath

In between bushwalks take the time to have a bit of a wander around the shops in Govetts Leap Rd and on the highway. One place not to be missed (even if you don't have much spare cash in your wallet) is the Victory Theatre Antique Centre in Govetts Leap Road. Opened in 1914 as the Arcadia Picture Palace and Skating Rink, this building is now an antique centre with over 30 stalls offering antiques, jewellery, books, collectibles, artworks and bric-a-brac.

Another place worth visiting, or maybe even attending for a weekend workshop, is Keith Rowe Glass (4787 7220), a glass-blowing studio and gallery located on the other side of the railway in the industrial units just past the Mitre 10 hardware store. Or, if you're feeling indulgent, the Jewel Blue Mountains Gallery in Govetts Leap Rd has an exquisite range of handcrafted jewellery, specialising in amber.

View from the Giant Stairway

Katoomba

Elevation: 1017 metres   **Population:** 8,000

Katoomba is the largest town in the Blue Mountains and, for many people, epitomises what the mountains is all about. There's a sense of grander times gone by, with splendid old hotels and faded street fronts, not to mention fine art-deco interiors, all set against the awesome backdrop of sheer cliffs, huge valleys and views stretching out for miles.

The main street itself is full of cafés, vintage clothing stores, second-hand books and antiques. Gone are the bright lights of Leura; instead there's a distinctly alternative vibe with backpackers, students, artists and the inimitable local residents. There's also a surprising amount going on: most weeknights and every weekend you'll find either live music or theatre at The Baroque nightclub and The Clarendon, not to mention other local venues such as The Carrington, The Gearins and The Savoy.

PUBLIC TRANSPORT

Local buses: Local buses leave from opposite the Carrington Hotel, at the top of Katoomba Street (www.bmbc.com.au, T 4751 1077).

Tourist buses: Tourist buses with unlimited day passes circuit South Leura and South Katoomba, passing near the beginning of most of the walks in this chapter. Contact Blue Mountains Explorer Bus (www.explorerbus.com.au, T 4782 1866) or Blue Mountains Trolley Tours (www.trolleytours.com.au, T 4782 7999).

Taxis: Phone 4782 1311 for the local taxi service.

This level track leads to a lookout with views of Mt Solitary, and is suitable for toddlers and grannies, wheelchairs and strollers.

The Skyway

At a glance

Grade: Very easy

Time: 15 minutes

Distance:
600 metres return

Weather: Suitable for all conditions

Closest public transport:
Local buses 686 and 696 run between Echo Point and Scenic World, stopping at Katoomba Falls Caravan Park

Finding the track

The track leads off from Cliff Drive, about 50 metres back from where Cliff Drive meets Katoomba Falls Road, at the reserve opposite Katoomba Falls Caravan Park. (See waypoint 5 on the map for walk 22 for more details.)

Lambertia formosa

Walk 19 A short walk for young children

Walk directions

1 Tea-tree bushes flank either side of the level path. Before long, you see the Skyway East station on your left. From here, a nail-biting cable-car swings over to Scenic World.

2 Keep going until you arrive at Cliff View Lookout, where you can enjoy views over to Mount Solitary straight ahead (known as Mun-mi-ee by the Gundungarra people) and to the Ruined Castle, on the ridge slightly to the right.

3 Return the way you came.

The track is level and easy

For families — Activities for Rainy Days

Oh no, you've been in Katoomba for over a week and it's *still* raining. The kids refuse to walk a single foot further and you're racking your brains for things to do. Here's a few suggestions:

- Do the whole railway/cableway/skyway number at Scenic World, Katoomba (www.scenicworld.com.au, T 4780 0200). Yes, it's a tourist trap, but the whole experience is kind of fun and at least you're out and about.

- Head for the Blue Mountains Aquatic Centre (www.bmcc.nsw.gov.au, Farnells Rd, Katoomba, T 4780 5156). There's an indoor pool, an outdoor pool (October to March), a sauna and spa and a fitness centre.

- Visit the Zig Zag Railway at Clarence and take a steam train along this historic railway line, www.zigzagrailway.com.au, T 6355 2955.

- Go to the movies. There's the Edge Cinema in Katoomba (www.edgecinema.com.au, T 4782 8900) or Mt Vic Flicks in Mount Victoria (www.bluemts.com/mountvic, T 4787 1577).

- Check out the NSW Toy & Railway Museum at Leuralla, Olympian Parade, Leura (www.toyandrailwaymuseum.com.au, T 4784 1169.) Leuralla features a toy museum (including a permanent Barbie Doll collection), a railway museum and five hectares of display gardens.

Didn't do enough walking during the day? Then try exploring Katoomba cascades at night. This walk is by no means a wilderness experience; rather it's a pretty silly and strange activity, but good fun nonetheless. Remember though — be back by 11 pm, as this is when the lights go out.

Finding the track

Head down Katoomba Street almost to the bottom, turning right into Katoomba Falls Road. This road curves down to the bottom of the hill, where you'll see Katoomba Falls Kiosk on your left. The track starts just a little to the right of the kiosk.

At a glance

Grade: Easy/Medium

Time: 30 minutes

Distance:
1 kilometre circuit

Weather: Easiest on a moonlit night

Closest public transport: As there are no local buses after dark, the closest public transport is Katoomba Railway Station, 2 km away

Walk directions

1 Descend concrete steps for 50 metres to the junction of three tracks. Go straight ahead, following signs to Reids Plateau.

2 Explore the rabbit warren of lookouts, where huge halogen beams shine over to the Three Sisters and also to Orphan Rock. At one lookout, a rather strange shelter shed, complete with picnic tables, offers shelter from wind and rain.

3 Return to the track junction and turn right, following the lights that illuminate the path as it winds down to the Duke and Duchess of York Lookout, which casts light down to Katoomba Falls.

4 The lights stop here but if there's any moon at all, you can follow the path down to the top of Katoomba Cascades, where the lights start again. (Alternatively, more pragmatic walkers may think to carry a torch.)

5 Cross the cascades and head up the steps, arriving at the south-eastern corner of the Cascades

picnic area in Katoomba Falls Road. There's a fascinating pollution-control device where the road crosses the top of the cascades, which captures stormwater debris before it hits the National Park.

6 From here follow the road back to the kiosk.

Out and about — The Edge Movie

If your legs are stiff from previous expeditions and you want to take it easy for a couple of hours, check out The Edge, a giant screen movie that features several times a day at The Edge Cinema in Katoomba. This well researched and beautifully filmed movie recounts the discovery of the prehistoric Wollemi Pine and flies you over waterfalls, through canyons and into inaccessible wilderness. Call 4782 8900 or visit www.edgecinema.com.au for times.

Orphan Rock at night

21 Picnics and play at Minnehaha Falls

This special track takes you through varied bush down to Minnehaha water hole, a place of significance to the women in the local Aboriginal community. This waterfall was christened in 1889 by a lover of Longfellow: "from the waterfall he named her Minnehaha — Laughing Water".

Side view of Minnehaha Falls

At a glance

Grade: Easy/Medium (some stairs)

Time: 1 hour 30 minutes

Distance:
2.7 kilometres return

Ascent/Descent:
90 metres ascent,
90 metres descent

Weather: Suitable for all conditions

Closest public transport: Local bus 697 goes to the corner of Minnehaha Road and Fifth Avenue, next to the start of the walk

Finding the track

On the northern side of Katoomba, follow Barton Street and then Minnehaha Road right to the very end. The walk starts to the left of the information board at the reserve car park area.

Walk 21 Picnics and play at Minnehaha Falls

Walk directions

1 The track leads off from the car park, turning sharply to the right before crossing Yosemite Creek on a sandstone causeway. On your left is a large hanging swamp, often lime-green with new growth.

2 Almost immediately, the firetrail forks. Straight ahead is the track to the falls; to the left, steps lead down to a small waterfall.

3 Gnarled scribbly gums line each side of the main track, silver-white in summer sun. Another sidetrack to the left leads down to a sandy picnic area, an ideal spot for children.

4 Over a shiny new footbridge, the path now continues high above the creekline. As the track starts to descend, take the short (unsignposted) detour to the left that branches off from the very first zigzag. This detour leads to an old lookout with a birds-eye view of Katoomba Creek. Be careful with children here, as around the lookout is quite exposed.

5 The main track descends steeply, with picture-perfect views along the way of Minnehaha Falls, encircled by sandstone cliffs. You soon arrive at the pool below the falls, a glorious spot. Take a break here before returning the way you came..

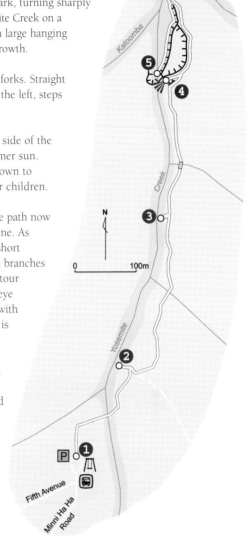

For families — Safe walking with children

The cliff walks in and around Katoomba are fairly level with fencing at most, if not all, lookouts. Parents with children still need to take care, of course, and in particular avoid letting younger children run ahead, as many sections of track are unfenced with relatively steep drops on one side or the other. If you're feeling anxious, the track leading from Scenic World to the Three Sisters (see Walk 22) is a good starting point, as it has better fencing than other clifftop walks in the area.

22 Walking the cliffs from Scenic World

With awesome lookouts at every turn, this easy walk connects Scenic World to the Three Sisters (Echo Point), two of the most visited tourist spots in the Blue Mountains. Well fenced and fairly level, this is the first stretch of the magnificent Prince Henry Cliff Walk (see also Walks 23 and 24).

Finding the track

Look for the three bronze maidens posturing outside the front of Scenic World. Immediately behind, a signpost indicates the start of the Prince Henry Cliff Walk.

Walk directions

1 At first, the track leads down between the main building and adjacent sheds. Follow the track straight ahead as it runs parallel to Cliff Drive.

2 After 250 metres, the Round Walk track goes down to your right. You can deviate around this loop if you like — it adds about half a kilometre and a 50 metre descent/ascent to the walk.

At a glance

Grade: Easy

Time: 1 hour 15 minutes

Distance:
2.3 kilometres one way

Ascent/Descent:
140 metres ascent,
110 metres descent

Weather:
Suitable for all conditions

Closest public transport:
Local buses 686 and 696 run between Echo Point and Scenic World every half hour. Special tourist buses also service Scenic World

The Three Sisters

Walk 22 Walking the cliffs from Scenic World

3 About 500 metres from Scenic World, you arrive at the reserve by Katoomba Falls Kiosk (a superior watering-hole, particularly for coffee aficionados). Head down the concrete steps to your right until you arrive at the junction of three tracks. Turn left (unsignposted), continuing along the Prince Henry Cliff Walk. Alternatively, a short diversion straight ahead leads to a couple of great lookouts of the Three Sisters and Orphan Rock.)

4 The track passes the Duke and Duchess of York Lookout before arriving at the rather polluted and weedy Katoomba Cascades. Steps lead up the right-hand bank, arriving at the reserve next to Cliff Drive. Turn right and walk through the reserve for 50 metres or so.

5 You'll see a large sign to Cliff View Lookout. The Prince Henry Cliff Walk continues from here. The next level section of track takes you to Cliff View Lookout, with views over to Mount Solitary and the Ruined Castle, and from there onto Wollumai and Allambie Lookouts. At Allambie Lookout, a simple bench carved into the rock under an overhang offers respite on a hot day. (Allambie is an aboriginal word meaning 'quiet place'.)

6 A short series of steps leads up to Lady Darley Lookout. Ignore the sidetrack leading up to Cliff Drive from the lookout and instead keep straight ahead, following signs to the Grand Cliff Top Track.

7 Before long, you emerge at the hubbub of the Three Sisters and Echo Point. From here, you can head back the way you came, catch a bus back to Scenic World or walk back through the streets along Cliff Drive.

This walk along the cliff tops combines great views, plenty of sitting spots, rainforest-gullies and lots of variety in the vegetation. The Solitary kiosk/restaurant two-thirds of the way along offers a spot for refreshments or alternatively, an earlier exit for those with weary feet.

Finding the track

From Katoomba Station, head down Katoomba Street to the bottom and follow signs to Echo Point/Three Sisters.

Walk directions

1 At Echo Point, enjoy the lookouts to the iconic Three Sisters. If it's quiet, try out the echo: face the west, give a long, loud 'coo-ee' and then wait. A couple of seconds later you should hear your call returning from the valley depths. After this demonstrative outburst, look for the archway to the left of the visitor centre and follow the concrete path that heads straight ahead.

2 After 350 metres, the track forks. Keep to the left, following signs for the Prince Henry Cliff Walk. A level sandy track leads you down to Lady Carrington Lookout, where even the ugly mesh fencing can't detract from the birds-eye view down into the Jamison valley.

At a glance

Grade: Easy/Medium

Time: 2 hours

Distance: 4.1 kilometres one way (includes sidetracks)

Ascent/Descent: 90 metres ascent, 170 metres descent

Weather: Suitable for all conditions, cooler in the afternoons

Closest public transport: Local buses 686 and 696 run between Echo Point and Scenic World every half hour. Special tourist buses also service Echo Point

Rock formations at Burrabaroo Lookout

Walk 23 Along the cliffs from the Three Sisters

3 From here, you carry on past Tallawarra Lookout (where a sidetrack leads back up to Cliff Drive), Honeymoon Point and Banksia Lookout (vegetated predominantly with casuarinas, not banksias).

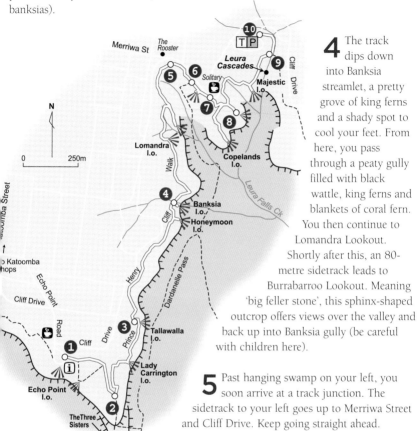

4 The track dips down into Banksia streamlet, a pretty grove of king ferns and a shady spot to cool your feet. From here, you pass through a peaty gully filled with black wattle, king ferns and blankets of coral fern. You then continue to Lomandra Lookout. Shortly after this, an 80-metre sidetrack leads to Burrabarroo Lookout. Meaning 'big feller stone', this sphinx-shaped outcrop offers views over the valley and back up into Banksia gully (be careful with children here).

5 Past hanging swamp on your left, you soon arrive at a track junction. The sidetrack to your left goes up to Merriwa Street and Cliff Drive. Keep going straight ahead.

Bands of ironstone

Tallawarra Lookout

By Banksia streamlet

Walk 23 Along the cliffs from the Three Sisters

6 After 100 metres or so, the Federal Pass leads down to your right, leading to Leura Forest (see Walk 34 to find out more). Ignore this track and keep going straight ahead. Shortly after this, a tiny sidetrack circles Echo Tree Lookout, where you can hear a clear echo bouncing off the opposite cliffs.

7 Now the track pops out at Cliff Drive. On your left, you'll see Solitary, an excellent café and upmarket restaurant. Walk along the road for a few metres and to your right you'll see a sign indicating where the track continues. Almost immediately, a sidetrack leads off to Copelands Lookout. This sidetrack adds 400 metres return to your trip, but leads to a quiet walled lookout with 300° views, a great picnic spot.

8 Back on the main track, another sidetrack takes you almost immediately to Bridal Veil Lookout. From here, the track winds around through cool rainforest, past the Round Walk junction that forks down to the right (keep straight ahead). Shortly after, a sidetrack to the right leads to Majestic Lookout.

9 A couple of minutes further on, steps lead

Honeymoon Lookout

down to a T-junction. To the right, Prince Henry Cliff Walk continues. Instead, turn left and follow the left-hand side of Leura Cascades until you emerge at the car park area.

10 From the car park, either return the way you came, walk back along the road (the road is shorter and quicker than the track), call a taxi or hop on a tourist shuttle bus.

For families — Toddlers in the bush

That couple of years when a child is too young to walk any distance, but too old to be carried, can be pretty frustrating for parents who are keen to get out and enjoy the bush. A possible compromise (albeit a rather tame one) is to take the Scenic Railway or Scenic Cableway ride down into the valley from Scenic World. From here, you can push a stroller along the kilometre or so of boardwalks as they wind through rainforest. Go after 3 pm and most of the tourist buses (and the associated tourists!) will already have left for the city. The last ride up the valley leaves at 4.45 pm.

24 The Prince Henry Cliff Walk

At a glance

Grade: Medium

Time: 4 hours

Distance: 8.8 kilometres (includes sidetracks)

Ascent/Descent: Gently undulating (380 metres ascent, 370 metres descent)

Weather: Fine weather is best to enjoy the views (avoid windy days)

Closest public transport: At the start of the walk, local buses 686 and 696 run to Scenic World from Katoomba railway station. At the end of the walk, local bus 695 runs past Gordon Falls Park. Special tourist buses also service both the start and end of the walk

Maps:
See Walks 22, 23 and 30

Almost 9 kilometres in its entirety, the Prince Henry Cliff Walk gives you a great sense of the Mountains landscape, with valley views, rainforest gullies and historic lookouts, not to mention the landmarks of Scenic World, the Three Sisters and Leura Cascades.

Finding the track

Look for the three bronze maidens outside Scenic World. Immediately behind, a signposted track leads down between the main building and adjacent sheds. This is the beginning of the Prince Henry Cliff Walk.

Walk directions

1 Follow the directions for Walk 22 (Scenic World to Echo Point). This is the most level and well-fenced section of Prince Henry Cliff Walk, with easy public transport at both ends.

2 Follow the directions for Walk 23 (Echo Point to Leura Cascades). This is the longest section out of the three, especially if you explore every sidetrack along the way. On hot summer days, you're best to do this walk in the cool of the afternoon when the sun has dropped behind the ridge.

3 Follow the directions for Walk 30 (Leura Cascades to Gordon Falls). This is the most protected from the sun out of the three sections, although many of the lookouts are very exposed and can feel quite precarious on a windy day.

For families — Managing the whinge factor

The Prince Henry Cliff Walk is a great walk for families, especially if you're not sure how long the kids will go for before they get exhausted or demand to be carried. You can exit the walk in about 20 different places, so when everyone has had enough, simply take the nearest exit and head back through the streets to your car, or use your mobile phone to call a taxi.

25 Descending the Three Sisters

This historic track was opened in 1932 after a long period of arduous construction, during which over 670 stone steps were carved into the side of the cliff with picks, hammers and chisels. Although the Three Sisters can be a busy spot, attracting more than 3 million visitors a year, the mob subsides as soon as you start to descend the Giant Stairway (910 stone steps and 32 steel staircases of almost vertical descent deter most tourists!)

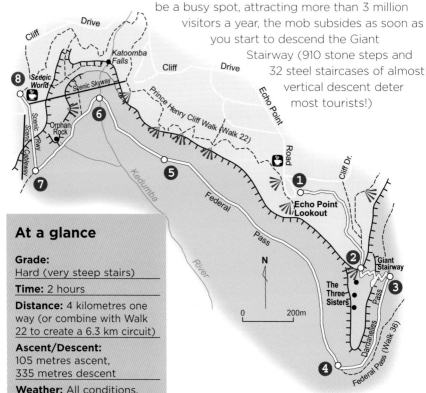

At a glance

Grade:
Hard (very steep stairs)

Time: 2 hours

Distance: 4 kilometres one way (or combine with Walk 22 to create a 6.3 km circuit)

Ascent/Descent:
105 metres ascent,
335 metres descent

Weather: All conditions, more sheltered in the afternoon

Closest public transport: Local buses 686 and 696 run between Echo Point and Scenic World every half hour. Special tourist buses also service Echo Point

Finding the track

From Katoomba Station, head down Katoomba Street to the bottom and follow signs to Echo Point/Three Sisters. The track starts at the stone archway just to the left of the Visitor Centre.

Walk 25 Descending the Three Sisters

Walk directions

1 Follow the concrete path that leads from the archway to the left of the Visitor Centre, signposted to the Three Sisters and the Giant Stairway.

2 Within five minutes, you arrive at Lady Game Lookout, with 180° views of the Jamison valley. From here, a staircase leads down to the bridge that crosses over to the First Sister and Honeymoon Cave. The steep descent begins, a combination of old sandstone steps (look for the old pick marks!) and newer steel staircases. Take your time here, and rest if your knees feel wobbly.

3 Before long, you arrive at the foot of the Giant Stairway, where you meet up with Dardanelles Pass. Turn right. Dardanelles Pass leads through sheltered forest, a mix of ferns, black wattles, vines and huge turpentines.

There are 898 steps down the Giant Stairway

4 After about 20 minutes, you join up with the Federal Pass, where finely crafted drystone walls offer a welcome sitting spot. Turn right, following signs to the Scenic Railway.

Walk variation

At the foot of the Giant Stairway, turn left along Dardanelles Pass instead of right. This diversion takes you to Leura Forest, at which point you can return along the Federal Pass (the Federal Pass and Dardanelles Pass run parallel to one another in this part of the forest). The Federal Pass joins up with Dardanelles Pass shortly after the Giant Stairway junction, and from here you continue straight ahead towards the Scenic Railway. This extra loop adds about 3 kilometres to the total distance. See Walk 36 for more details.

Walk 25 Descending the Three Sisters

5 As you progress along the Federal Pass, the forest thickens, with more and more turpentines dotting the sides of the path, ragged bronze-brown trunks towering high overhead. As the rainforest vegetation increases, the larger leaves block sunlight, making the understorey thinner.

6 A kilometre or so along the Federal Pass and and you arrive at Cooks Crossing, where Katoomba creek winds over a jumble of mossy jagged boulders. This is where you a couple of picnic benches as well as find the first (and last!) swimming holes on this walk. (These pools are small and rocky, okay for cooling off but not really deep enough for swimming.)

7 Soon after you start to hear the hubbub of the Scenic Railway. At this point, you can either take a quick ride up the hill with the Scenic Railway or follow the boardwalk just a little further to the Cableway station.

8 You arrive at Scenic World. From here, you can catch public transport to your next destination, or follow the Prince Henry Cliff Walk (see Walk 22) back to Echo Point.

The Scenic Railway

NO ENTRY

Federal Pass

Walk variation

This walk only explores one section of the Federal Pass. If you'd like to make more of a day of it, you can continue beyond the Scenic Railway (waypoint 7 on the map for this walk), exploring the landslide and the lush rainforest environment that lies below the escarpment. After three kilometres, you arrive at the Golden Stairs track junction (see waypoint 8 on Walk 27 for details). The Golden Stairs take you up on to Narrow Neck (Glenraphael Road), from where you can either walk back along the road, or, if reception is available, use your mobile phone to call a cab.

Scenic World boardwalk

Mountains environment — Mapping the land

Even though most walkers love and respect the bush around them, the land is generally thought of as something separate to people. In contrast, Aboriginal elders will tell how their people didn't make a distinction between themselves and the land in which they live: the land, animals, plants and people are all one entity. As part of this, many Aboriginal people have unique perceptions of birth and death, believing that their own spirits have existed since the Dreamtime, living in the land that is their origin. Just as ancestral spirits shaped the land, marking out special places, travel maps and sacred places, so does the spirit of each Aboriginal person, as they create their own spiritual 'map' of the land around them.

26 Narrow canyon of Devil's Hole

Although this walk (indeed, some may call it a scramble) is very steep, rocky and at times difficult to follow, Devils Hole is a dramatic and rewarding walk. Leading through a narrow cleft in the cliff walls between Boars Head Rock and Narrow Neck, the track follows a route originally used by the Gundungurra people coming up from the Megalong Valley and, much later, by miners from the Glen Shale Mine village.

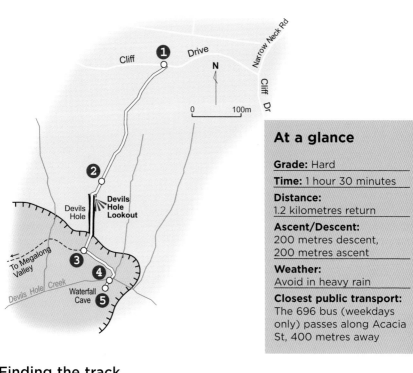

At a glance

Grade: Hard

Time: 1 hour 30 minutes

Distance:
1.2 kilometres return

Ascent/Descent:
200 metres descent,
200 metres ascent

Weather:
Avoid in heavy rain

Closest public transport:
The 696 bus (weekdays only) passes along Acacia St, 400 metres away

Finding the track

Head down Katoomba Street almost to the bottom, turning right into Katoomba Falls Road. This road becomes Cliff Drive and winds around for another 3 kilometres or so. The track to Devils Hole begins opposite no. 239 Cliff Drive, where a steel pole and a new NPWS sign mark the start of the walk.

Walk directions

1 Head down the eroded track, watching your step on the uneven ground. To your left, scrub opens up to a hanging swamp dotted with slender Blue Mountains Ash. Look at your surroundings carefully; you want to be confident that you'll recognise this track on your return journey.

A stand of Blue Mountains ash

2 After 250 metres or so the track veers slightly to the left and starts to descend steeply down the gorge. An overhang on your right offers a rather damp resting place. The chasm overhead narrows and at the right time of day, light shafts down, magnifying water droplets and drifting pollen. Further along, suspended high above, hangs a boulder wedged between the two cliff walls.

3 After 15 minutes or so of fairly difficult descent, the gorge widens. A red marker on your right indicates where the track does a final zigzag down the hill, past ferns and over thick leaf litter. A couple of minutes further on, a NPWS sign marks the track junction. At this point, you could either turn right or left. The track to the right leads to the Megalong Valley, but for the purpose of this walk go left, following the faint track that hugs the base of the escarpment.

4 After two minutes, you'll see a waterfall straight ahead (or if it's raining, you'll actually see a smaller waterfall followed by a larger waterfall). At this point, you again have a choice. There is a muddy track that passes right underneath the larger of the two waterfalls, but this route is somewhat exposed and a slip would be nasty. Alternatively, you can pick your way over boulders to cross the waterfall at its base.

5 Just beyond the second waterfall, right up against the cliff wall, you arrive at Waterfall Cave, a large flat overhang that's a favourite spot with climbers. Rest and enjoy before heading back up the way you came.

Walk variations

From Waterfall Cave, a climber's track follows the base of the escarpment for another couple of kilometres (beware: the Water Board ladders up Narrow Neck are now closed). Or, for a full-day walk, return to the foot of the gorge (waypoint 3) and head straight ahead, turning right onto the old Water board service road and then right into Nellies Glen Road, following the Six Foot Track back up to West Katoomba (topographic map required).

27 Historic Federal Pass

This walk descends Furbers Steps and joins up with the Federal Pass, opened on January 1st 1901 in honour of the federation of Australian states. A long but relatively easy-going day, most of this walk passes along the sheltered forest floor before popping out at the Ruined Castle, where 360° views offer a sense of being 'on top of the world'.

Finding the track

Head down Katoomba Street almost to the bottom, turning right into Katoomba Falls Road. This road curves down to the bottom of the hill, where you'll see Katoomba Falls Kiosk on your left.

Walk directions

1 The track starts just a little to the right of the kiosk. Descend concrete steps for 50 metres to the junction of three tracks. Head to your right, following signs for Katoomba Falls Track.

2 About 10 minutes further on, past the Witches Leap waterfall, you arrive at the Round Walk junction. Turn left onto the Furbers Steps Track, following signs to the Federal Pass. These steps lead past Rainforest Lookout, Queen Victoria Lookout and Furbers Lookout. (Ignore sidetracks to Underfalls Walk and Veras Grotto.)

At a glance

Grade: Very Hard

Time: 7 hours

Distance:
14.4 kilometres return

Ascent/Descent:
370 metres ascent,
370 metres descent, plus
12 kilometres of
undulating track

Weather:
Suitable for all conditions

Closest public transport:
Local buses 686 and 696 run between Echo Point and Scenic World, stopping at the Katoomba Kiosk where the track begins

Claystone ledge, foot of Furbers Steps

Furbers Steps

3 While descending Furbers Steps, look for pick marks in the stone, evidence of where these steps were blasted from the cliff in 1908. Levelling out a little, the clay-floored track undercuts sandstone overhangs before arriving at the Federal Pass. Turn right.

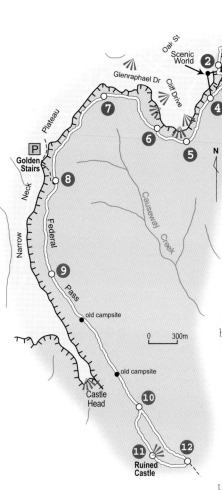

4 A few minutes further on, the inevitable crowd of tourists assemble at the foot of the Scenic Railway. Apparently the steepest in the world, this incline railway was constructed in the late 1800's to haul shale and coal out of the valley, but by 1932 was already a tourist attraction. Just past the Scenic Railway the track forks; stick to the right, ignoring the Scenic World boardwalk, following signs to the Landslide.

5 About ten minutes further on, 60 metres past where steel cables cut across the track, you'll see a faint pad veering off to the left — this is the Williams' Landslide Deviation, a more direct but rather indistinct route to the Golden Staircase. Ignore this track; keep going straight ahead.

6 An exposed coal seam marks the first of the landslides, opening up to the massive landslide caused by mining activities which fell on three separate dates during 1931. Steel poles painted yellow mark the route across bare rocks and water-scoured gullies. Beyond the landslide, the track widens, with drystone embankments evidence of the old horse-drawn tramway which led to the Ruined Castle mines.

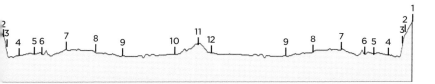

Walk 27 Historic Federal Pass

View over to Narrow Neck and Ruined Castle

7 About 600 metres from the end of the landslide, just beyond a small creek crossing, look for the mine shaft recessed into the bank on your right-hand side. This is the Mt Rennie Tunnel, through which coal was transported from the Megalong Valley under Narrow Neck along a cable tramway.

8 Another kilometre of level walking and you arrive at the track junction where the Golden Stairs descends from Narrow Neck (an alternative entry/exit point for this walk). Keep straight ahead.

9 The vegetation changes as you continue through the forest: tall tree ferns give way to a long grove of coachwoods, later opening up to a tall forest of blue gums, angophora and black ash. Lyrebirds scratch underfoot and bellbirds ring all around. There are several old miners' campsites along this stretch, as well as the ruins of an old hut.

10 About 45 minutes (2.5 kilometres) from the Golden Stairs junction, turn right at the sign to the Ruined Castle. A steep, rocky ascent leads to the top before you head south-east along the spine of the ridge.

11 The broken shapes of the crags at Ruined Castle make it easy to understand the origin of its name, when back in 1880 a journalist described it as a 'rocky pile the ruined keep of some gigantic castle'. The highest point is at the southernmost end, just before the track starts to descend. A short scramble delivers 360° views: north to Castle Head, south to Warragamba, east to Kings Tableland, and west to Narrow Neck, where the headwaters of Cedar Creek appear as twin waterfalls.

12 The track descends back down to the Federal Pass. Turn left. After 600 metres you arrive at the original sign leading up to Ruined Castle. Return the way you came. (If you're planning to catch the Scenic Railway up the hill, remember the last one leaves at 4.50 pm.)

The Ruined Castle

Old miners' campsite

Mountains history — Narrow Neck Landslide

On 18 June 1929, local miner Arthur Mellor came across a crack running along the top of Dog Face Rock. The crack was only 20 centimetres wide but was extraordinarily deep, exceeding 120 metres in depth. The next day the crack had widened a further 25 centimetres and that week continued to widen dramatically, causing curious crowds to gather as they waited for the 'mountain to fall apart'.

The landslide itself happened in January 1931, when a huge piece of Dog Face bluff splintered from the cliff, crashing into the valley below. Curiously enough, no one in Katoomba witnessed the landslide although Myles Dunphy (a tireless campaigner for wilderness and national parks) was camping near Oberon at the time and reported hearing 'a terrific detonation'.

One theory for the cause of the landslide is that when props were removed from abandoned mines, some of which tunnelled underneath Dog Face and through Narrow Neck, the whole escarpment weakened. However, this phenomenon of huge sandstone blocks breaking off along vertical joint planes of weakness is what drives the vertical retreat of the cliff faces in the Blue Mountains, giving the area its special character and appearance.

Sublime Point at sunset

Leura

Elevation: 985 metres   **Population:** 4,400

Arriving at Leura Mall on the weekend can be a bit of a culture shock: luxury 4 wheel drives fighting for parking spots, smart Sydneysiders bursting out of cafés, expensive boutiques competing against cutesy homeware outlets. The backdrop to this retail paradise is an olde-world landscape of European trees and landscaped gardens, with an array of weatherboard holiday cottages, federation guesthouses and swish hotels.

Surrounding all this hustle and bustle are some of the finest walks in the Blue Mountains. On the south side of Leura you'll find waterfalls, rainforest tracks and splendid cliff walks, not to mention the ancient Aboriginal occupation shelters at Lyrebird Dell. On the north side, you'll find exposed and pristine heathland, abundant wildflowers and views to make your heart miss a beat.

PUBLIC TRANSPORT

Local buses: Local bus 695 leaves from Leura Mall (next to the train station), providing access to all walks that start near York Fairmont Resort and at Gordon Falls (www.bmbc.com.au, T 4751 1077).

Tourist buses: You can buy unlimited day passes on tourist buses that circuit South Leura and South Katoomba, passing by Gordon Falls, Leura Cascades and Scenic World.

Contact Blue Mountains Explorer Bus (www.explorerbus.com.au, T 4782 1866) or Blue Mountains Trolley Tours (www.trolleytours.com.au, T 4782 7999).

Taxis: Phone 4782 1311 for the local taxi service.

28 A sublime lookout

At the end of a suburban street, a short walk delivers 270° views, framed by Kings Tableland to the east and the Three Sisters to the west, with Mt Solitary and Narrow Neck Plateau completing the picture.

Finding the track

From Leura railway station, follow Railway Parade in an easterly direction. Take the seventh turn on your right (Gladstone Road), the fifth on your left (Fitzroy Street) and follow the dog-leg as it turns into Sublime Point Road. The track starts at the very end of Sublime Point Road.

Walk directions

1 Take the gently graded path down to a little picnic hut, and from here follow the steps down to where the lookout perches on the nose of the ridge. Beyond the Three Sisters, you can see how Narrow Neck Plateau connects with Mt Solitary, with the Ruined Castle appearing as a little bump between the two. On a clear day, you can see as far as Bimlow Walls, 29 kilometres away.

2 Return the way you came.

At a glance

Grade: Easy

Time: 15 minutes

Distance: 400 metres return

Weather: Best on a clear day

Closest public transport:
Local bus 695 goes as far as Fitzroy St (weekdays only). From here, it's 2 km down Sublime Point Road to the track's start

View from Sublime Point

29 Creeks and pools at Lyrebird Dell

This walk makes for an easy circuit with lots of variety. The temperature drops as you descend into a pocket of rainforest and the waterfall at the Pool of Siloam. From here you follow the creek around to Lyrebird Dell, a significant cultural feature where evidence of Aboriginal occupation dates back over 12,000 years.

At a glance

Grade: Easy

Time: 1 hour

Distance:
1.4 kilometres circuit

Ascent/Descent:
70 metres descent,
70 metres ascent

Weather: Shady and sheltered; perfect for hot or windy days

Closest public transport:
The Explorer Bus, the Trolley Tours bus and local bus 695 all drive along Gordon Road, past the beginning of this walk

Finding the track

From Leura railway station, head south down Leura Mall, taking the fourth road on the left (Gordon Road). At the end of Gordon Road, turn right into Lone Pine Avenue and continue until you come to the reserve. There are some public toilets, an electric BBQ and a small parking area.

Walk directions

1 The track starts 50 metres beyond the toilets on the eastern side of the reserve. Follow signs to the Pool of Siloam and Lyrebird Dell and head down towards the creek, over shady steps and underneath dripping sandstone ledges.

The Pool of Siloam

Walk 29 **Creeks and pools at Lyrebird Dell**

2 At the first fork in the path, head to your right down to the Pool of Siloam. This pool used to be so deep you would have had to dive to reach the bottom, but over recent decades the surrounding developments and poor erosion control have caused the pool to silt up. After enjoying the pool, head back up to where the path forked and turn right, following signs for the Lyrebird Dell. Follow the left-hand side of the creek, past the gully filled with king tree ferns.

3 Once at a narrow metal bridge cross over to the right-hand side of Gordon creek and continue along the track, sticking to the creek line and ignoring sidetracks leading up to your right.

4 After another five minutes or so you come to a large overhang — this is the first of two Aboriginal occupation caves. Around the corner you'll come across the second shelter cave, complete with a flat, grassy area and insensitively placed picnic tables. Cross another metal bridge, with the cascades on your right. Active bush regeneration is slowly healing the weed problems caused by the old sewage line that used to pass through here.

5 The path climbs steeply for a short distance before popping out in the reserve behind Leura Oval. Turn left and head along the dirt track.

6 After 300 metres you arrive at Lone Pine Avenue. Continue along the avenue back to the reserve where the walk started.

Mountains history

At Lyrebird Dell excavations in the larger of the two overhangs (next to the picnic tables) and the discovery of several hundred stone flakes (flakes are produced during the manufacture of tools, such as axe-heads) have revealed a continuous history of Aboriginal occupation going back over 12,000 years. There is also some pigment in the area near the occupation shelter. It's easy to see how much climatic conditions must have changed over this time — even in drought conditions, the surrounding hanging swamp renders the shelter continually moist and impractical as a shelter.

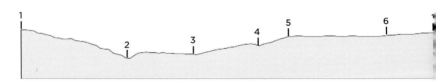

Walk variations

Instead of going on the Lyrebird Dell circuit, you can continue past the Pool of Siloam up to Golf Links Lookout, a quiet spot with views stretching miles into the valley. From here, you can either return the way you came or wander up to Gladstone Street and back through the sleepy streets of South Leura.

Picnic tables at Lyrebird Dell

Mountains environment

All around the Blue Mountains you'll see the distinctive trunk and foliage of grass trees (otherwise known as xanthorrheas). If you see a large grass tree, then chances are you're looking at a very old plant — a grass tree can grow for up to 600 years, with the trunk taking over 20 years to develop.

Grass trees have an enormous array of uses. Aboriginal people used to soak the flower spikes in water, so that the nectar from the flowers would create a sweet-tasting drink. The spike itself can be used for making spears and also as the drill base for making fire (rubbing a smaller stick in the hollow centre to create friction). The spiky leaves can be woven into containers, and the resin from the trunk used as a glue. Parts of the grass tree can also be used for medicinal purposes.

30 Rainforest, cascades and lookouts

This last section of the Prince Henry Cliff Walk connects with Walks 22 and 23 to create a complete journey along the escarpment between Katoomba and Leura. The most sheltered of the three sections, the track from Leura Cascades offers cool, fern-filled gullies, pockets of rainforest and a series of lookouts with uninterrupted views of the Jamison valley.

Finding the track

From Leura railway station, head down Leura Mall and take the fifth road on your right, Gordon Road, which shortly after becomes Cliff Drive. Follow Cliff Drive around for about a kilometre until you see a sign to Leura Cascades on your left. This side road loops down to the Leura Cascades parking area.

At a glance

Grade: Easy

Time: 1 hour 30 minutes

Distance:
2.4 kilometres one way

Ascent/Descent:
110 metres descent,
150 metres ascent

Weather: Fine weather is best to enjoy the views (avoid windy days)

Closest public transport: The Explorer and Trolley Tour tourist buses stop at both Leura Cascades and Gordon Falls Park. Local bus 695 also runs past Gordon Falls Park

View from Gordon Falls Lookout

Walk directions

1 At the parking area, a quirky archway and shelter mark the beginning of the Leura Cascades Track. Head off down the right-hand side of the creek.

2 After about 200 metres, cross left over a wooden footbridge. Keep going straight ahead, following signs for the Prince Henry Cliff Walk. Only a couple of minutes past the footbridge, a gravel area to the side of the track and an old timber tower mark where a Flying Fox once carried materials down to the sewer works in the valley.

3 At the next track junction (about 15 minutes further on), take the sidetrack to your right, signposted to Bridal Veil Falls. This longish detour (350 metres return) takes you to an isolated outcrop with a view to the first drop of Leura Falls (often called Bridal Veil Falls). To the left of the falls, the ragged cliff face is shaped like outstretched fingers. From here, return to the track junction and go straight ahead to continue along the escarpment.

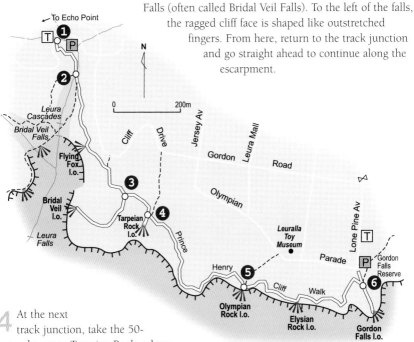

4 At the next track junction, take the 50-metre detour to Tarpeian Rock, where layers of ironstone make wizened shapes in rock platforms. From here, the track ascends a little, winding past old picnic benches tucked under ledges overgrown by ferns, before zigzagging back up.

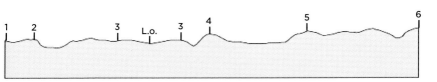

5 A short distance takes you to Olympian Lookout (unsignposted). Ignore the track leading back up to Olympian Parade and keep going straight ahead, past another lookout (unsignposted), over the bizarrely ugly Buttenshaw Bridge, and on to Elysian Lookout. Look for the large mountain devils (Lambertia formosa) with their spiky leaves and clusters of red flowers, grouped in sevens.

6 Shortly further on, you arrive at Gordon Falls Park. The track ends here, but take one last detour down the steps to your right. At the lookout, look right around to your left for views of Gordon Falls.

Mt Solitary in the distance

For families

If you don't live in the bush or go bushwalking often, one of the questions you may want to ask is whether the walks in this book are safe. In the Blue Mountains, the answer is that there isn't a single walk that can be guaranteed as childproof — even the wheelchair-friendly Fairfax Track in Blackheath culminates in a lookout (albeit fenced) with a 180-metre drop below. However, the key to bushwalking safety with children is supervision. With one child and two adults, almost any walk in this book is possible, and arguably quite safe. With thirty children and one adult, you'd be crazy to try even the easiest walk in this book.

Probably the best advice is to start with the easy walks and see how you (and your children) fare. If you decide to try one of the harder grades, make sure you have lots of time and at least one adult per child.

Bridal Veil Falls

31 An easy walk to Moya Point

Starting at the golf course by York Fairmont Resort, a shady track winds down through ferns, sedges, banksias and tea-trees, leading first to Gladstone Lookout and then to Moya Point. These lookouts are both bare, exposed spots but Moya Point in particular is a special spot to watch the sun set (just remember to take a torch with you to find your way back home).

Finding the track

From Leura railway station, follow Railway Parade in an easterly direction. Take the seventh turn on your right (Gladstone Rd) and follow the signs to the York Fairmont Resort. Head down to Level 4 of the resort car park.

Walk directions

1 On the eastern side of the car park, take the unsignposted track that leads across the edge of the golf course, heading past the tennis courts and through a wooded area.

2 About 350 metres from the car park, at the 14th tee, signs indicate the start of the Inspiration Point track. Descend gradually through banksias, bloodwoods and boronias.

At a glance

Grade: Easy

Time:
1 hour 30 minutes

Distance:
2.7 kilometres return

Ascent/Descent:
70 metres descent,
70 metres ascent

Weather:
Suitable for all conditions

Closest public transport:
Local bus 695 goes as far as Fitzroy St (weekdays only). From here, it's 800 metres down to the resort car park

View from Gladstone Lookout

3 Another 200 metres further on the track forks: head right, continuing on the Inspiration Point Track.

4 Half a kilometre further on, take the track to your right, signposted to Gladstone Lookout.

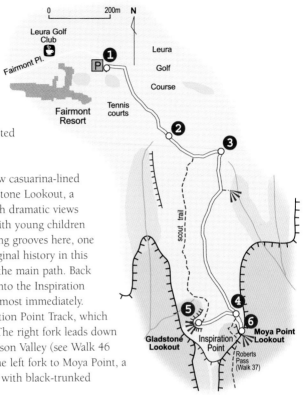

5 Before long, this narrow casuarina-lined path pops out at Gladstone Lookout, a bare, unfenced lookout with dramatic views across the valley (careful with young children here). There are axe-grinding grooves here, one of the many signs of Aboriginal history in this area. From here, return to the main path. Back at waymark 4, turn right onto the Inspiration Point Track, which forks almost immediately. Turn right onto the Inspiration Point Track, which forks almost immediately. The right fork leads down Roberts Pass into the Jamieson Valley (see Walk 46 for details). Instead, take the left fork to Moya Point, a rocky, exposed spot dotted with black-trunked xanthorrheas (grass trees).

6 From here, look to the left to see the distinctive amphitheatre shape of Wentworth Falls. From Moya Point, return to the car park the same way you came.

Walk variations

The 'scout trail' offers an alternative route from Gladstone Lookout back to the golf course, making for an interesting and more adventurous circuit (note: the track is rather overgrown and indistinct in places). The trail starts about 30 metres back from the Gladstone Lookout and follows the southern edge of the escarpment, treating the walker to continuous glimpses of Mt Solitary before joining up with the main track, just before the golf course.

101

32 The wild landscape of Fortress Rock

A quiet sandy trail with flannel flowers, native irises and boronias leading to an exposed and lonely lookout. Unsignposted and not widely known, this is a favourite spot with locals.

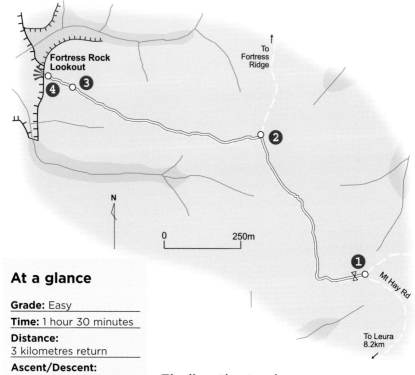

At a glance

Grade: Easy

Time: 1 hour 30 minutes

Distance:
3 kilometres return

Ascent/Descent:
80 metres ascent,
80 metres descent

Weather: Avoid in very misty or windy weather

Closest public transport:
Leura railway station,
8.8 kilometres away

Finding the track

From the Great Western Highway in Leura, follow Mount Hay Road as it turns from suburbia and bitumen to dirt track and heath. At 8.2 kilometres from the highway you'll see a rocky fire trail leading up to your left with a small sign saying Fortress Ridge.

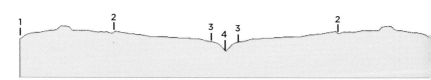

Walk 32 The wild landscape of Fortress Rock

1 Go straight up the hill, past the locked gate. Occasionally you'll see swamp wallabies next to this trail, peeking out from the low vegetation.

2 After 700 metres the fire trail forks. Keep to your left. Observant eyes may notice that further on a faint track leads off to your right, winding down to a gully and around to Dark's Cave. Rumour has it that Eric Dark, husband of novelist Eleanor Dark, used to take his family to this cave for weekend retreats, and apparently also used it to train volunteer defence forces during World War II. For the time being, ignore this sidetrack (if you spot it) and keep straight ahead.

3 You arrive at a small turning circle where the fire trail ends. At the right time of year, you'll see carpets of flannel flowers all along here. Keep going, following the rocky track that leads downwards for about 100 metres.

4 The track comes to a rather undefined end,

View from Fortress Rock

perched on an exposed and rocky outcrop (a truly terrifying spot for parents with children). From here you can see the Blackheath skyline, with the Grose Valley opening up below. After enjoying this wild and lonely view, return the way you came.

Sidetrack to Dark's Cave

Walk variation

On your return, instead of returning to your car, head off to your left at the junction of the two fire trails. After 500 metres the fire trail turns to the right, down to Fortress Creek but a footpath goes straight ahead, following Fortress Ridge. Explore this track as far along the ridge as you have energy (it goes for another 3 kilometres or so) and then return the way you came.

Grand cliff top track to Wentworth Falls

The Grand Cliff Top Track follows the cliff tops from South Leura to Wentworth Falls. More sheltered than the Prince Henry Cliff Walk that extends from Leura to Katoomba, this track offers lots of variety: long boardwalks crossing over hanging swamps, sidetracks to plunging lookouts, ferny nooks and deep gullies, not to mention the Conservation Hut offering refreshments at the walk's end.

Finding the track

From Leura railway station, follow Railway Parade in an easterly direction. Take the seventh turn on your right (Gladstone Rd) and follow the signs to the York Fairmont Resort, which is at the northernmost end of Sublime Point Rd. The track starts from Level 4 of the resort car park.

Walk directions

1 On the eastern side of the car park, take the unsignposted track that leads across the edge of the golf course, heading past the tennis courts and through a wooded area.

2 About 350 metres from the car park, at the 14th tee, a partially hidden moss-covered sign indicates the start of the Inspiration Point track. Descend gradually through banksias, bloodwoods and boronias.

At a glance

Grade: Easy/Medium

Time: 1 hour 30 minutes

Distance: 2.3 kilometres one way

Ascent/Descent: 110 metres descent, 125 metres ascent

Weather: Suitable for all conditions, quite special in the mist

Closest public transport: For the beginning of the walk, local bus 695 goes as far as Fitzroy St, 800 metres from the resort car park. At the walk's end, local bus 685 goes from Fletcher Street (next to the Conservation Hut) all the way to Wentworth Falls railway station

Picnic table near National Pass junction

Waratah in full bloom

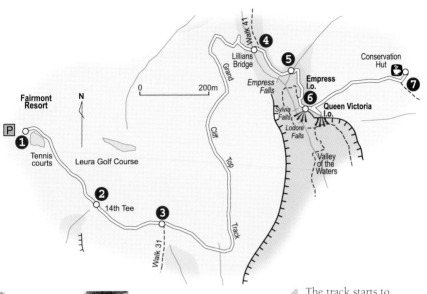

3 Another 200 metres further on the track forks. Keep left, following the Grand Cliff Top Track signs. (The track to the right forms part of Walk 31 to Moya Point and Gladstone Lookout.) After a few minutes, long, elegant boardwalks cross the hanging swamp. There's lots of birdlife here, especially in the early morning.

Boardwalks across hanging swamp

Walk variation

For a longer walk, turn left at Lillian's Bridge and follow the Nature Track in reverse (see Walk 41) up to West Street (the point at which you can see the Great Western Highway). From here, walk through the streets of South Leura back to the Fairmont.

4 The track starts to descend into Lillian's Glen and arrives at Lillian's Bridge, perched high above the canyon. Cross the bridge and turn right.

5 Shortly you'll pass a damp gully and picnic bench on your left, where two Blue Mountains ash trees tower overhead. Over a simple footbridge and the track joins with the National Pass coming up from the valley. Fork up to your left. At the end of an eroded claystone ledge, three sets of steep metal steps provide a stiff cardiac workout.

6 From Empress Lookout you can see Empress Falls tumbling down the narrow canyon opening. A minute or so later, take the small sidetrack to Queen Victoria Lookout, where you can look far into the Jamison Valley. Continue uphill. Soon, the Overcliff Track branches off to the right, followed shortly by the Shortcut Track. Keep straight ahead.

7 The Conservation Hut, with its open fireplace and comforting hot drinks, makes a welcome sight.

Footbridge near National Pass junction

Mountains environment — hanging swamp

On many of the Leura walks (such as Lockley Pylon, Fortress Rock, the Grand Cliff Top Track and sections of the Prince Henry Cliff Walk), you'll see large areas of hanging swamp. You can recognise these swamps as grass-like clearings between areas of eucalypt woodland, often perched around headwaters of creeks or balanced on cliff edges. Hanging swamps form on the rock surfaces and clay soils underneath, and common swamp plants include button grass, coral fern, hakea, melaleuca and sedges. The rich diversity of swamps and surrounding habitats attracts many birds, insects and mammals.

Hanging swamps are a very significant part of our eco-system because of the way they regulate water. Not only do hanging swamps filter ground water (thereby helping to reduce siltation and pollution), but when it rains, the swamp plants absorb water like a huge sponge, only releasing this water again when dry weather comes. Along creek lines this means that the swamp regulates the flow of water of the creek and hence the waterfalls that the creek feeds.

There are some plants (such as *Microstrobus fitzgeraldi*) that only exist in the spray of waterfalls in the Upper Mountains. When a hanging swamp is damaged, this water-regulating effect is diminished, meaning that in dry weather, the spray of the waterfalls covers a smaller area. When poorly planned development destroys areas of hanging swamp, this has the potential to cause a species several kilometres away to become extinct.

34 Wildflowers and wind at Lockley Pylon

This track has a remote and sometimes bare feeling about it, which belies the enormous variety of vegetation and birdlife encountered as you wander across hanging swamp, over low heathland and through sheltered woodland patches. The walk culminates at Lockley Pylon, a conical-shaped peak with 360° views.

At a glance

Grade: Medium

Time: 3 hours

Distance:
7.8 kilometres return

Ascent/Descent:
160 metres ascent,
160 metres descent

Weather: Best in fine weather with little wind. Avoid full summer sun.

Closest public transport: Leura railway station, 11 km away.

Finding the track

From Leura railway station, head right onto the Great Western Highway and then first left into Mt Hay Road. Follow Mt Hay Road for 10.4 kilometres (the road turns into dirt after 2 kilometres but it's fine for a two-wheel drive). You'll see a sign on your left indicating the start of the track to Lockley Pylon.

Walk directions

1 Follow the track across the hanging swamp. After about five minutes, the track forks. Stay left (the right-hand fork explores the rock formations and comes back to join the main track a little further on). The wonderful thing about this stretch of bush is the variety — from any single spot you'll see at least ten different species.

The rocky, sandy track leading to Lockley Pylon

2 Along this stretch, you'll see three rock formations on your right, extending for 500 metres or so. These formations are called The Pinnacles and over millions of years the wind has worn away some of the softer rock, leaving layers of brittle iron stone and creating the tessellated shapes that look like waves.

3 The vegetation changes and you pass through a kilometre or so of low scribbly gums with an understorey of wildflowers. Look out for the sweet-smelling boronias and deep red waratahs in early spring, along with carpets of eriostemon. There's also an abundance of persoonia (geebung) from which the berries, at the right time of year, make excellent bush tucker.

4 The track briefly gains at Mount Stead with views over the swamp and down to Fortress Creek, a popular spot with canyoners. From here the track descends through another short but sheltered stretch.

5 Change course here, bearing westwards across a bleak and treeless terrain. The track forks at the foot of the cone-shaped Lockley Pylon, named after John Gilmour Lockley, a journalist and conservationist who publicised the Blue Gum forest campaign in 1932. Bear left, heading for the top.

6 From the top of Lockley Pylon you can see straight ahead (southeast) to Pulpit Rock in Blackheath. The cliff to your left (south) is Fortress Ridge. To the west is Govetts Leap and Horseshoe Falls, with Govetts Creek winding its way down to the Grose River. The distinctive shape of Mt Hay is to the north-east. After taking in these extraordinary views, return the way you came.

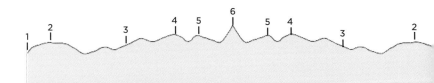

Walk variations

The track that continues past Lockley Pylon continues for almost another kilometre down a short steep gully, over a creek bed and around to some rocky lookouts, arriving at Du Faur Head. From here, you can return back to Lockley Pylon or alternatively, take the track that heads steeply down to the Blue Gum forest below. From here several exits out of the Blue Gum are possible, including Perry's Lookdown in Blackheath (see Walk 18).

Lockley Pylon

Out and about — Everglades Gardens

For garden-lovers, the Everglades in Leura make for a tranquil place to spend a couple of hours. Created in the 1930s by famed designer Paul Sorenson, the Everglades is one of Australia's most famous heritage gardens. Elaborate sandstone terraces, sweeping lawns and 12 acres of European-style landscapes sit against a backdrop of native bush and escarpment views. Address: 37 Everglades Avenue, Leura. T 4784 1938. Adults: $7. Children: $3.

This ideal summer walk descends past Leura Cascades to the foot of Bridal Veil Falls, follows the amphitheatre track around, and then ascends up Fern Bower (part of the original Federal Pass) before arriving at Solitary (a great place to snack and recuperate). A short stretch along the road then takes you back to Leura Cascades.

Finding the track

From Leura railway station, head down Leura Mall and take the fifth road on your right, Gordon Road, which shortly after becomes Cliff Drive. Follow Cliff Drive around for about a kilometre until you see a sign to Leura Cascades on your left. This side road loops down to the Leura Cascades parking area.

At a glance

Grade: Hard

Time: 1 hour 45 minutes

Distance:
2.5 kilometres circuit

Ascent/Descent:
220 metres descent,
220 metres descent

Weather:
Perfect in warm weather

Closest public transport:
The Trolley Tours and Explorer tourist buses drive past Leura Cascades every 30 minutes or so

Tree ferns flank the track

Walk directions

1 From the archway and National Parks noticeboard, head off down the right-hand side of the creek, following signs for the Leura Cascades Track.

2 After about 100 metres, cross over a wooden footbridge, ignoring the Prince Henry Cliff Walk that branches off in either direction. Continue down the left-hand side of Leura Falls Creek for another 150 metres before arriving at a viewing platform of the base of Leura Cascades. Cross the creek again.

3 After several flights of steps, you arrive at the unsignposted Evelyn Lookout. Just past this lookout the track forks. Straight ahead is the Round Walk that circles back to Leura Cascades. Head down to your left, following signs to Cliff Drive via Fern Bower. From here, a series of steep steps lead down through a cool, dark rainforest dotted with hundreds of rough tree ferns.

4 The track opens up briefly at the foot of the snout-shaped Bridal Veil Falls, then ascends to McKillop's Lookout before arriving at a secluded stretch called the Amphitheatre, where spray drips from above and king ferns thrive in the protected grotto.

5 Past the Amphitheatre, the track opens up again. Looking down, you get more of a sense of how this track is perched on a narrow band of claystone halfway down the cliff face. Be careful with children here and watch your step.

6 At the next track junction, continue straight ahead, following signs to the Prince Henry Cliff Walk. The track follows Linda Creek up a fern-filled gully, protected by a canopy of tall coachwood and sassafras. Sheltered from drying wind and summer heat, the forest is lush here, with moss-covered boulders shining an almost iridescent green. You may think the ladders here

are steep, but think back to the original bushwalkers in 1890, who navigated this ascent using a series of precarious bush pole ladders.

7 You emerge at Jamieson Lookout, followed shortly afterwards by the junction of the Prince Henry Cliff Walk and the Federal Pass. From here, turn right and follow the Prince Henry Cliff Walk for

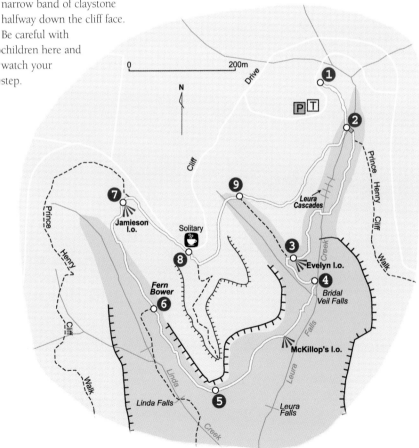

Walk variation

Instead of walking along the road between Solitary and Leura Cascades, you can go along the Prince Henry Cliff Walk. For more details, follow waypoints 7 to 10 from Walk 23 (Along the cliffs from the Three Sisters).

100 metres until it emerges onto Cliff Drive.

8 On your left, you'll see Solitary, an excellent café and upmarket restaurant. Walk along the bitumen for a few metres and to your right you'll see a sign indicating where the track continues. Almost immediately, a sidetrack leads off to Copelands Lookout. (This sidetrack adds 400 metres return to your trip, but leads to a quiet walled lookout with 300° views, a great picnic spot.) Back on the main track, another sidetrack takes you almost immediately to Bridal Veil Lookout.

9 The track passes the Round Walk junction. Continue straight ahead. You soon arrive back at waypoint 2, near the beginning of your walk. Head left back up to the car park area.

Footbridge by Leura Cascades

Out and about — Craft markets

If you're in the Mountains on the first Sunday of the month, check out Leura Craft Markets, held at Leura Public School (on the corner of the Great Western Highway and Mt Hay Road). A mostly local selection of homemade jams, crafts, paintings and plants make a change from the retail glories of mainstream Leura.

36 Picnics and train rides on the Federal Pass

This walk descends past Leura Cascades to the foot of Bridal Veil Falls, and then continues to Leura Forest and along the Federal Pass to the foot of the Scenic Railway. A great day out, this walk has everything: historic tracks, waterfalls, views and rainforest. Best of all, when you're tired out at the end of the day, there's a train ride back up the hill (last train leaves 4.45 pm).

At a glance

Grade: Hard

Time: 3 hours

Distance: 5.25 kilometres one way (feels like more!)

Ascent/Descent:
260 metres descent,
320 metres ascent
(including train!)

Weather:
Perfect in warm weather

Closest public transport:
Trolley Tours and Explorer tourist buses service both Leura Cascades and Scenic World every 30 minutes or so. Local buses 686 and 696 also service Scenic World

Finding the track

Head down Leura Mall and take the fifth road on your right, Gordon Road, which shortly after becomes Cliff Drive. Follow Cliff Drive around for about a kilometre until you see a sign to Leura Cascades on your left. This side road loops down to the Leura Cascades parking area.

Walk directions

1 From the archway and National Parks noticeboard, head off down the right-hand side of the creek, following signs for the Leura Cascades Track.

2 After about 100 metres, cross over a wooden footbridge, ignoring the Prince Henry Cliff Walk that branches off in either direction. Continue down the left-hand side of Leura Falls Creek for another 150 metres before arriving at a viewing platform of the base of Leura Cascades. Cross the creek again.

Historic shelter shed

3 After several flights of steps, you arrive at Evelyn Lookout (unsignposted) where the cliffs on either side frame a perfect view of Mt Solitary. Just past this lookout the track forks. Straight ahead is the Round Walk that circles back to Leura Cascades. Head down to your left, following signs to Cliff Drive via Fern Bower. From here, a series of steep steps lead down through a cool, dark rainforest dotted with hundreds of rough tree ferns.

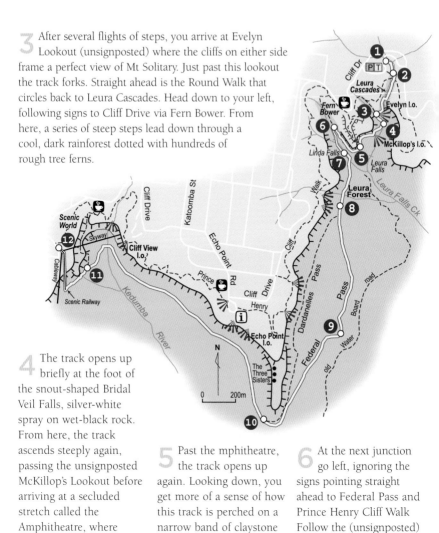

4 The track opens up briefly at the foot of the snout-shaped Bridal Veil Falls, silver-white spray on wet-black rock. From here, the track ascends steeply again, passing the unsignposted McKillop's Lookout before arriving at a secluded stretch called the Amphitheatre, where spray drips from above and king ferns thrive in the protected grotto.

5 Past the mphitheatre, the track opens up again. Looking down, you get more of a sense of how this track is perched on a narrow band of claystone halfway down the cliff face. Be careful with children here and watch your step.

6 At the next junction go left, ignoring the signs pointing straight ahead to Federal Pass and Prince Henry Cliff Walk Follow the (unsignposted) track as it heads steeply down, crossing Lila Falls.

7 Only a short distance further on, cross Linda Creek again at Linda Falls. If you have time on your hands, you may want to explore the faint sidetrack that leads off to your left just after Linda Falls. This was the route of the original Federal Pass, from where the Tunnel Track ascended to the Amphitheatre and the Lindeman Pass continued all the way to Wentworth Falls. However, the main track continues its descent.

8 Leura Forest is 300 metres further on. Huge boulders splintered from the escarpment thousands of years ago created a ledge in which fertile soil has built up, allowing rainforest plants to flourish. The thick canopy includes turpentines, coachwoods and sassafras. The shelter shed here was originally constructed in 1893 and rebuilt in 1991. Two tracks run almost parallel to one another from the southern side of the forest. The upper track is Dardanelles Pass, which leads directly to the Giant Stairway, and the lower of the two is the Federal Pass. Follow signs to continue along the Federal Pass.

9 After a kilometre or so, you may spot the old water board service

The Federal Pass

road way down on your left. This whole stretch of track is much quieter than the tracks leading down to Leura Forest, and if you're quiet, you'll often see (or hear) lyrebirds scratching in the rainforest.

10 Almost two kilometres after leaving Leura Forest, Dardanelles track rejoins the Federal Pass. Continue straight ahead along the Federal Pass for another two kilometres. The track gets busier again but is still very pretty, flanked with salmon-bark angophoras, gnarled tree roots and turpentines. At Cook's Crossing the track crosses Kedumba River, with views of the base of Katoomba Falls.

11 A couple of minutes further on, signs point to Furbers Steps (an alternative way back up the cliff if you're feeling either very energetic or a bit short of cash). Keep going for another few minutes until a cacophony of screams, squealing brakes and the clicking of cameras herald the arrival of what is the 'steepest railway in the world', as it descends 200 metres in less than half a kilometre.

12 Join the railway for a hysterical ride up to Scenic World, where the walk ends.

Lodore Falls, Valley of the Waters

Wentworth Falls

Elevation: 866 metres   **Population:** 5,650

Wentworth Falls may not have the majestic bleakness of Blackheath, the hippy-feral charm of Katoomba or the glitzy shopping of Leura but nonetheless, it's an attractive village with some of the most spectacular walks in the Blue Mountains. Even better, the walks are not quite as deluged with tourists as they are in many other places — go midweek or early in the morning, and you'll be able to enjoy most of the walks in relative solitude.

Comparing the delights of these walks is impossible — they're all wonderful in their own way. However, if you have time for a three hour walk and don't mind a steep slog uphill at the end, then don't miss Walk 44, the National Pass. It's quite simply fantastic.

PUBLIC TRANSPORT

Train: Wentworth Falls train station is 2.5 km away from Wentworth Falls Picnic Area, where most of the walks begin. The Charles Darwin Trail (see Walk 39) starts close to the station and follows the creek all the way to the Picnic Area.

Taxis: Phone 4782 1311

Buses: Blue Mountains Bus Company (www.bmbc.com.au, T 4751 1077)

37 View from Princes Rock

This gently graded walk leads to a parapet lookout with views of Kedumba Walls, Kings Tableland, Mt Solitary and Sublime Point. For the early risers, it's the perfect place to watch the sun come up.

Kedumba Walls

At a glance

Grade: Easy

Time: 30 minutes

Distance: 1 kilometre return

Weather: Views are best on a fine day

Closest public transport: Local bus 685 runs past the corner of Fletcher St and Falls Rd, 500 metres from Wentworth Falls picnic area

Map: For more details, see the map for Walk 42

Finding the track

From Wentworth Falls railway station, turn right onto the Great Western Highway and then first left into Falls Road. Follow Falls Road for 1.7 kilometres to very end, and then follow signs to your right down to Wentworth Falls Picnic Area.

Old drinking trough

Walk directions

1 From the car park area, walk 150 metres along the tarred road to Wentworth Falls Lookout. You'll see a sign on your right indicating the start of the Princes Rock Track.

2 Head down gradually through a variety of vegetation. You'll see an old drinking trough carved into the rock on your left, sculpted by the original makers of this track. (These days, the water probably isn't safe to drink however!)

3 After 10 minutes of steady descent, you arrive at the old parapet lookout, where locals like to sit and paint, watch the sunset, even get married occasionally. To your left, you can see Wentworth Falls, with its 180-metre high drop. The ridge that runs south from the Falls is Kings Tableland, and the cliff walls (called Kedumba Walls) provide one of the sheerest drops anywhere in the mountains. Ahead is the distinctive shape of Mt Solitary and to your right you can see Sublime Point.

4 Head back the way you came.

Wentworth Falls

Walk variations

As you're facing uphill towards the Picnic Area a few metres back from the lookout, a track leads down to your left. This track leads a short distance down to the Undercliff Track (see Walk 42). At the Undercliff Track junction, you can either turn left to head towards the top of the falls or right to head towards Den Fenella and the Overcliff Track.

Kings Tableland Aboriginal Site is highly significant to the Darug, Wiradjuri and Gundungarra people. Used as a gathering place for at least 14,000 years, the area contains a variety of cultural features, including engravings, axe-grinding grooves, modified rock pools and an occupation shelter. The place has a desolate beauty and a timelessness that is hard to describe.

View from Kings Tableland rock platform

At a glance

Grade: Easy

Time: Allow 1 hour to explore

Distance: 1 kilometre return

Weather:
Suitable for all conditions

Closest public transport:
Wentworth Falls railway station, 4.1 km away

Finding the track

From Wentworth Falls railway station, head east along the Great Western Highway for 2 kilometres and turn right into Tablelands Road. Go straight ahead for 1.6 kilometres, turning left into Queen Elizabeth Drive. The track starts 500 metres down this road, about 100 metres after the last house on the left-hand side. (Note: precise access details are subject to change due to a long-running dispute regarding land ownership next to the last house.)

Walk directions

1 From where the bitumen ends walk down the road for about 100 metres.

2 Just before the road curves slightly to the left, you'll see a faint sandy track (unsignposted) leading up to your right. Follow this track over the rocks for another 100 metres until you meet an old fire trail.

3 Turn right and after only 50 metres, head left on a sandy track that leads up to a rock platform, with the main platform opposite to the left. The striking tessellated formation of this platform, with deep ridges like a reptile's skin, is thought to be related to glacial activity that occurred between 18,000 and 30,000 years ago.

4 Next to the first information sign, follow the somewhat overgrown track leading down to your left until you arrive at an occupation shelter where deposits date back about 22,000 years. If you look carefully, you can see engravings of bird and macropod tracks, as well as a half circle (an unusual motif not known at any other location in the Greater Blue Mountains). Be careful not to let any part of your body or clothing brush against the walls of the shelter.

5 Head back up to the main rock platform. There are over 150 axe grinding grooves on this platform and in the immediate vicinity. Aboriginal people would sharpen tools by dipping them in water and then grinding the edge against the groove of the rock.

6 Before your return, enjoy the views extending to Bowral in the south and to Sydney CBD in the east.

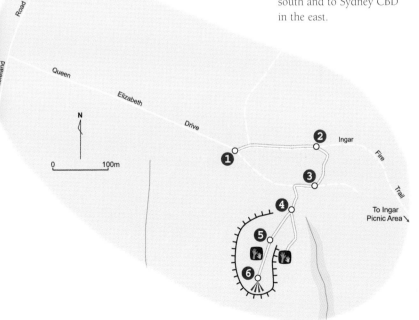

39 Charles Darwin Trail

In 1836, Charles Darwin walked from the Weatherboard Inn along Jamison Creek to the cliff's edge to where 'an immense gulf unexpectedly opens through the trees, with a depth of perhaps 1,500 feet'. The track was formally opened in 1986 and now leads from Wentworth Falls train station all the way to the top of Wentworth Falls. Lots of bridges, shallow waterholes, boardwalks and sheltered overhangs make this an ideal family walk.

At a glance

Grade: Easy

Time: 1 hour 30 minutes

Distance: 3.1 kilometres one way

Ascent/Descent: 70 metres gradual descent, 80 metres ascent

Weather: Suitable for all conditions

Closest public transport: Wentworth Falls railway station is 300 metres from the start of the walk. Local bus 685 runs past the corner of Fletcher St and Falls Rd, 500 metres from the picnic area where the walk ends

Finding the track

From Wentworth Falls railway station, turn right onto the Great Western Highway and then turn left into Falls Road at the first set of traffic lights. On your left, you'll see a play park and tennis courts. In the park, adjacent to the tennis courts, is a large sign indicating the beginning of the Darwin Trail.

Walk directions

1 Follow the track as it meanders along next to the creek. The houses on either side thin out, the radiata pines and weeds become fewer and the lush hanging swamp takes hold. You soon pass the Water Board road on your left, opposite a rusty overhead pipeline.

Steps leading down from tennis courts

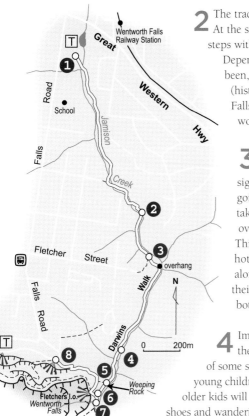

2 The track crosses the creek several times. At the sixth crossing there's a set of steel steps with a wooden bridge below. Depending on how much rain there's been, this is a decent waterhole (historically, this was the Wentworth Falls Swimming Baths, complete with wooden changing sheds).

3 Ten minutes further on, ignore a sidetrack on the right, signposted to Fletcher Street. Keep going straight ahead until a few steps take you down to a large rock overhang next to a small waterfall. This makes a great picnic spot in hot weather. From here, continue along the creek. Boardwalks pick their way through banksia, boronia, bottlebrush, dog rose and tea-tree.

4 Immediately after the last boardwalk there's a little beach area at the foot of some small cascades — a lovely spot for young children to paddle and play. Slightly older kids will probably enjoy taking off their shoes and wandering downstream along the creek itself, exploring rock pools and ledges and looking for yabbies.

5 Only a couple of minutes further along the track there's a fork. The main track veers up to the right, signposted to the Picnic Area. Ignore this track and instead stick left, staying on the narrower track that follows the creek. From here, a set of steel steps takes you to the bottom of Weeping Rock, a wide set of cascades surrounded by lots of shallow pools.

Walk variations

The Charles Darwin Trail takes you to the start of many of the walks mentioned in this book, including Rocket Point, Undercliff/Overcliff Walk, the National Pass and Wentworth Pass.

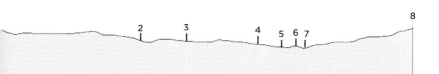

Walk 39 Charles Darwin Trail

The Charles Darwin Trail

6 Continue beyond Weeping Rock and you arrive at a well-signposted track junction. The landscape opens up all of a sudden, or as Darwin wrote, 'one stands on the brink of a vast precipice and below one sees a grand bay or gulf … thickly covered with forest'. Turn left, following signs to Wentworth Falls.

7 After a short descent you'll arrive at the top of Wentworth Falls. Don't be tempted to step over the barrier here — over the years, several foolhardy tourists have lost their lives this way. After enjoying the view, head back up the way you came, up as far as the first junction. Head left and then almost immediately turn right, heading directly up the hill, following the signs back up to the Picnic Area.

8 The track emerges at Wentworth Falls Lookout. From here, you can either return the way you came or walk back along Falls Road to the Great Western Highway.

The view at the top of Wentworth Falls

Out and about

If discovering the wonders of nature during the day isn't enough, Kings Tableland Observatory in Wentworth Falls offers a chance to look at the wonders of the sky at night. Facilities include three modern telescopes as well as a flat screen planetarium for cloudy nights. Opening hours are Friday, Saturday and Sunday from 7pm (8pm during daylight saving), or every night in the school holidays. 55 Hordern Road, T 4757 2954.

40 Wentworth Falls and Rocket Point

This escarpment track takes you past Fletchers Lookout and down to the top of Wentworth Falls. From the Falls, a quiet circuit leads to Rocket Point from where you get a bird's-eye view of just how narrow the ledges are, and how the Undercliff Track and the National Pass cling to the cliff face.

At a glance

Grade: Easy/Medium

Time: 1 hour

Distance:
1.9 kilometre circuit

Ascent/Descent:
110 metres descent,
110 metres ascent

Weather:
Suitable for all conditions

Closest public transport:
Local bus 685 runs past the corner of Fletcher St and Falls Rd, 500 metres from the picnic area

Finding the track

From Wentworth Falls railway station, turn right onto the Great Western Highway and then first left into Falls Road. Follow Falls Road for 1.7 kilometres to very end, and then follow signs to your right down to Wentworth Falls Picnic Area.

Walk directions

1 From the car park area, walk 300 metres along the tarred road to Wentworth Falls Lookout, where a large sign indicates the start of the Wentworth Falls and National Pass tracks.

2 Follow the signs to the National Pass, heading downhill. Turn right at the first fork, following signs to Wentworth Falls. Look to your left at this junction to see filtered views of Weeping Rock.

The top of Wentworth Falls

Walk 40 **Wentworth Falls and Rocket Point**

3 At the base of some steps you come to a T-junction (with Fletchers Lookout straight ahead). Turn left and then continue straight ahead following signs at each juction to Wentworth Falls and the National Pass. Steps lead down to the top of the falls, where you cross Jamison Creek on stepping stones.

4 About 20 metres further on, signs on your left indicate the start of Rocket Point circuit. Head up here. The track forks again almost immediately — take the right fork to follow this circuit anti-clockwise.

5 The narrow rocky track heads steeply up to a tunnel-like shelter gouged between huge rocks (an excellent spot to shelter from sun and rain). From here, a short sidetrack to your right leads to the old parapet construction at Rocket Point Lookout. From here, return to the main track, hugging the edge of the cliff line as the track winds steadily uphill. There's an abundance of birdlife and wildflowers here in spring, including swathes of fragrant boronias.

6 After a short distance the track forks once more. Keep left to stick to the Rocket Point circuit. The track now winds around to follow the creekline back to where the Rocket Point circuit began. Return the way you came, across the top of the Falls and back up to the Picnic Area.

Fletcher's Lookout

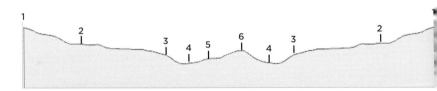

Walk variations

Where the track forks after Rocket Point Lookout (waypoint 6), you can head uphill to your right (rather than continuing on the Rocket Point Circuit). This sidetrack pops out at the end of Hordern Road. From here, it's about an extra kilometre to Kings Tableland Aboriginal Site (see Walk 38).

View from Rocket Point

The Nature Track is one of those walks you can whiz around in an hour, or alternatively explore for half the day. Heathland views, hidden pools and fern-lined creeks make for many lovely diversions along the way.

Finding the track

From Wentworth Falls railway station, turn right onto the Great Western Highway and then first left into Falls Road. Follow Falls Road for 1.3 kilometres and take the third street on your right (Fletcher Street). Follow Fletcher Street for a further 800 metres right to the very end to the car park next to the Conservation Hut café.

Walk directions

1 The track starts just to the right of the café, next to the old toilets, and is clearly signposted. Follow the level sandy track northwards. After 10 minutes or so the track bends to the left (ignore the rocky track leading up to your right).

2 300 metres further on, a signpost indicates the start of the Nature Track. Head left, away from the noise of the highway and down towards the creek.

At a glance

Grade: Medium

Time: 1 hour 45 minutes

Distance:
3.1 kilometre circuit

Ascent/Descent:
210m descent,
210m ascent

Weather: Suitable for all conditions

Closest public transport:
Local bus 685 runs along Fletcher St and Valley Road, 200 metres from the Conservation Hut.

Asmosdeus Pool

Walk 41 Secluded pools on the Nature Track

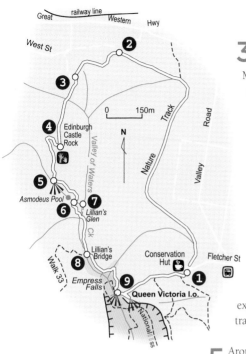

3 At the T-junction a few minutes later, turn left again. Metal steps lead across a large expanse of hanging swamp, with a variety of sedges, grevilleas, tea-trees and hakeas. This is great place for bird watching, especially early in the morning.

4 Another 300 metres and you arrive at Edinburgh Castle rock, a platform of eroded rock formations with views to the east. Aboriginal axe-grinding grooves are hidden away on rocks surrounded by the low vegetation of dwarf banksia and tea-tree. After exploring, continue along the main track, heading down to your right.

5 Around a bluff and an exposed outcrop treats you to wind, silence and 180° views. Look down to where Valley of the Waters canyon cuts its way towards Empress Falls. The track curves around slightly and then descends steeply through a cool, fern-lined gully.

6 At Lillian's Glen (marked by old concrete stepping stones crossing a small creek), a short scramble upstream to your right leads to the dark, mossy and rather mysterious Asmodeus pool, where light filters down from the canyon above.

7 Back on the main track you soon come to another creek crossing. If time allows, leave the track again and head up to your left to the junction of two creeks. A few metres paddle up the right-hand tributary reveals a flight of steps carved into the side of a waterfall, leading to the old Flora baths at the top (be careful, these steps are very slippery with no handrail and a big drop, very unsuitable for children).

Walk 41 Secluded pools on the Nature Track

8 A little further along the main track is Lillian's Bridge, perched high above the narrow Valley of the Waters canyon. Don't cross this bridge but instead continue. Shortly you'll pass a damp gully and picnic bench on your left, where two Blue Mountains Ashes perennially shed their ribbon-shaped bark. After a simple footbridge the track joins with the National Pass coming up from the valley. Fork up to your left.

9 A few minutes further on and three sets of metal ladders offer a free cardiac workout, leading up to Empress Lookout, followed shortly afterwards by Queen Victoria Lookout. One final slog uphill, ignoring tracks branching off to your right, and you're back at the Conservation Hut for a well-earned cuppa.

Walk variations

Instead of passing Lillian's Bridge, cross over and follow the Grand Cliff Top Track to Leura Golf Course. See Walk 33 for more details.

Steps leading up to Flora's Bath

For families

Several of the Wentworth Falls walks (Undercliff Track, Overcliff Track, National Pass and Wentworth Pass) offer the choice of starting either at the Picnic Area or the Conservation Hut. If you're walking with children, you're best to start at the Picnic Area and finish up at the Conservation Hut, so that the walk ends (rather than starts) with a café, giving the kids a destination to aim for. If they're really tuckered out, one of the adults can even scoot across to the Picnic Area and drive back to the Conservation Hut to pick everyone up.

Steps back up to the Hut

42 Cliff Top Circuit
(Undercliff, Overcliff, Shortcut Tracks)

There's a maze of tracks around the top of Wentworth Falls, all of which you can mix and match to create different walks. This circuit takes in some of the best of this area's scenery, without having to descend too far into the valley. Two sidetracks along the way (the first at Den Fenella, the second at Breakfast Point) offer early exits should you run out of steam.

At a glance

Grade: Medium

Time: 2 hours

Distance: 3.5 kilometre circuit

Ascent/Descent:
150 metres ascent,
150 metres descent

Weather:
Suitable for all conditions

Closest public transport:
Local bus 685 runs past the corner of Fletcher St and Falls Rd, 500 metres from the picnic area.

Finding the track

From Wentworth Falls railway station, turn right onto the Great Western Highway and then first left into Falls Road. Follow Falls Road for 1.7 kilometres to very end, and then follow signs to your right down to Wentworth Falls Picnic Area.

Walk directions

1 From the car park area, walk 300 metres along the tarred road to Wentworth Falls Lookout. Straight ahead you can see Mt Solitary (over 7 kilometres away) and to your right, Sublime Point. Following signs to Wentworth Falls Track, head downhill.

2 After a further 300 metres, there's a fork in the track where if you look to your left, you can see filtered views of Weeping Rock. Turn right, following signs to Wentworth Falls.

View across to Mt Solitary

Walk 42 Cliff Top Circuit

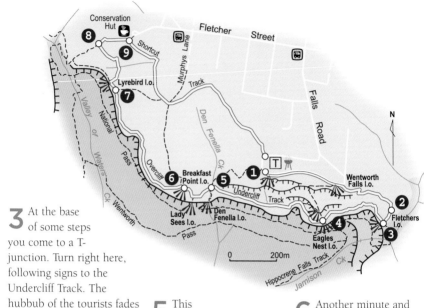

3 At the base of some steps you come to a T-junction. Turn right here, following signs to the Undercliff Track. The hubbub of the tourists fades almost immediately as this old track picks its way over a narrow sandstone ledge, with dripping overhangs above and boggy ground and swamp underfoot.

4 350 metres further on, a sidetrack to the unmarked Eagles Nest lookout provides an eyrie's view of the Jamison valley. Early and late in the day, clouds and tall escarpments cast huge shadows over vegetation that stretches as far as the eye can see. Continue past the lookout.

5 This sheltered stretch of bush arrives at a wooden footbridge and the Den Fenella track junction. For an extra diversion, head to your left down to the Den Fenella lookout where the creek tumbles down into an amphitheatre-shaped gully (about 15 minutes return). Otherwise, keep going straight ahead, along what is now the Overcliff Track. From here, the track climbs steeply for a couple of minutes. A sidetrack (currently unsignposted) to the left leads to Lady Sees lookout.

6 Another minute and you arrive at Breakfast Point lookout, a rocky outcrop from where you can see the junction of Jamison Creek and the Valley of the Waters creek in the valley below. Ignore the unsignposted track leading back up the hill; instead keep going straight ahead, following the cliffline.

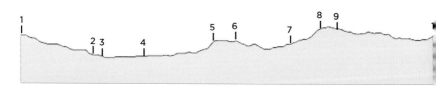

The sheltered Undercliff Track

7 Deep orange cliffs give way now to moist hanging swamp with coral fern, button grass and swamp grevillea. It's muddy and damp underfoot here, especially after rain. A few more minutes and you arrive at Lyrebird Lookout. Keep straight ahead and, at the unsignposted fork in the track a couple of minutes further on, bear right.

8 The Overcliff Track joins the Valley of the Waters track coming up from the valley. Turn right, following signs to the Conservation Hut.

9 Just before the top, with the Conservation Hut in sight (you may want to pop up here for a quick refreshment) there's a sign on your right to the Shortcut Track. Turn right here and follow this level, shady track until it pops out at the Wentworth Falls Picnic Area where you began.

43 Creeks and cliffs to the Conservation Hut

This walk combines two local favourites. The first leg is the Charles Darwin walk, which follows Jamison Creek from Wentworth Falls railway station all the way to the top of the Falls themselves. The second leg follows the Undercliff and then the Overcliff Tracks that connect the Falls to the Valley of the Waters.

Finding the track

From Wentworth Falls railway station, turn right onto the Great Western Highway and then turn left into Falls Road at the first set of traffic lights. On your left, you'll see a play park and tennis courts. In the park, adjacent to the tennis courts, is a large sign indicating the beginning of the Darwin Trail.

At a glance

Grade: Medium

Time: 2 hours 30 minutes

Distance:
5.3 kilometres one way

Ascent/Descent:
90 metres descent,
100 metres ascent

Weather: Suitable for all conditions

Closest public transport: Wentworth Falls Railway Station is 300 metres from the start of the walk. At the walk's end, local bus 685 runs past the corner of Fletcher St and Valley Rd, 200 metres from the Conservation Hut

Maps: See walks 39 and 42

View across Kedumba Walls

Walk 43 Creeks and cliffs to the Conservation Hut

Out and about

Wentworth Falls lake is a great spot for picnics and gatherings. Not only is there a big expanse of water surrounded by bush (with a little ingenuity, you can walk around the lake, although the path runs out after a while), but there's also a couple of barbeque hotplates, two kids' play areas (including a pretty good pirate ship) and a dozen unique sandstone sculptures. A couple of small beaches at the northern end offer the best swimming, a languid delight in the late afternoons of summer. To get to the lake, head north from Wentworth Falls railway station, over the railway bridge and then turn first left into Sinclair Crescent. The lake is about 400 metres further on.

Steps back up to Conservation Hut

Walk directions

1 Follow the instructions for Walk 39 up until waypoint 7, where you arrive at the top of Wentworth Falls.

2 After enjoying the view, head back up the way you came. At the first junction, turn left and keep going straight ahead, following signs to the Undercliff Track. You are now at waypoint 3 on the map for Walk 42.

3 Follow the instructions for Walk 42 right to the end, as the Undercliff Track turns into the Overcliff Track and finally emerges at the top of the Valley of the Waters and the Conservation Hut.

For families

One of the stressful things about walking with toddlers or young children in the Blue Mountains is the precipitous drops that seem to lurk around every corner. Wentworth Falls is no exception — almost every walk offers views that gladden the hearts of most, but reduce parents of young children to a nervous wreck. Although parents need to take care towards the end of the walk (both at Weeping Rock and at the lookout just above the falls), the Charles Darwin Trail (Walk 39) offers a great compromise. The track is mostly very level (although unsuitable for strollers) and runs alongside a creek, where there are lots of spots for children to paddle safely in the water and explore the surrounding bushland.

44 The National Pass

Distant views, stone steps hewn into the side of the sandstone cliffs, waterfalls, ferny grottos and swimming holes all combine to justify the reputation of the National Pass as one of the Blue Mountain's classic walks. The only downside is the popularity of the track — it's hard to experience wilderness with twenty earnest backpackers trudging past. Go early in the day, or if you can, midweek outside school hols, to enjoy this walk at its best.

Finding the track

From Wentworth Falls railway station, turn right onto the Great Western Highway and then first left into Falls Road. Follow Falls Road for 1.7 kilometres to very end, and then follow signs to your right down to Wentworth Falls Picnic Area.

Walk directions

1 From the car park area, walk 300 metres along the tarred road to Wentworth Falls Lookout, where a large sign indicates the start of the National Pass walking track.

At a glance

Grade: Hard

Time: 3 hours

Distance:
4.8 kilometres circuit

Ascent/Descent:
210 metres descent,
210 metres ascent

Weather:
All conditions, even a delight in mist and rain

Closest public transport:
Local bus 685 runs past the corner of Fletcher St and Falls Rd, 500 metres from the picnic area.

Cliff walls in the mist

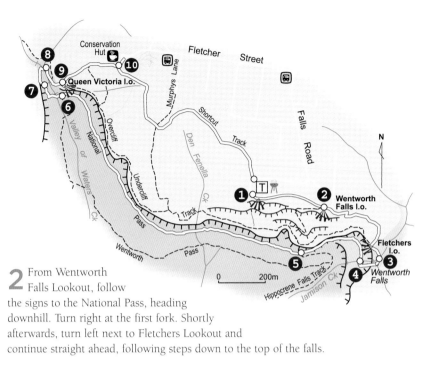

2 From Wentworth
Falls Lookout, follow
the signs to the National Pass, heading
downhill. Turn right at the first fork. Shortly
afterwards, turn left next to Fletchers Lookout and
continue straight ahead, following steps down to the top of the falls.

3 Cross the top of the falls on stepping stones. (Careful here after rain and don't be
tempted to explore on the other side of the fence.) After a short level stretch, the
track descends steeply down a series of sandstone steps built by Peter Mulheran and a
group of men called 'The Irish Brigade' in 1908 and restored by National Parks 100
years later, in 2008. (If you're scared of heights, go slowly and keep looking at the
steps, not the view!)

4 At the bottom, the track recrosses Jamison Creek immediately below the first
drop of Wentworth Falls. This is a great spot to rest, looking up at the first
110-metre drop of the falls. From here, zigzag westwards, hugging the base of the
cliff.

5 Ignore the turnoff to Wentworth Pass and Slacks Stairs and keep going straight
ahead. You're now walking along a claystone ledge perched halfway down the
cliff, ducking under ledges and dodging the spray of waterfalls. As you continue, the
cliffs close in on either side.

6 About 40 minutes after crossing the falls, as you approach the Valley of the Waters, ignore the track that comes up from your left — this is Wentworth Pass joining again with the National Pass (see Walk 45). Continue uphill. Shortly afterwards, cross the Valley of the Waters creek at the base of Lodore Falls, again on stepping stones.

7 Head uphill past Sylvia Falls where the water fans out like a veil, always seeming to catch the light, regardless of the time of day. A few minutes further on you cross one last time at the base of Empress Falls (a sublime swimming hole for those who don't mind the cold).

8 Continue on, heading up two sets of simple wooden steps and across a side creek. At the next junction, fork to the right uphill, following signs to the Conservation Hut.

9 More steep steps lead past Empress and Queen Victoria Lookouts. Looking down, you can see the 'open' eucalypt forest of

The top of the National Pass descent

the Jamison Valley, so called because the canopy is relatively sparse and only blocks out 35 to 70 percent of the sky. The Conservation Hut café finally appears on the horizon (making an excellent diversion and resting spot).

10 Just a few metres below the Conservation Hut, the Shortcut Track branches off. This sandy, sheltered track heads directly back to the Picnic Area car park.

Walk variations

If you're travelling by public transport, you can create a more extended walk by starting at Wentworth Falls railway station and heading along the Darwin Trail (see Walk 39) until you arrive at the top of the falls.

45 Ladders and forests of Wentworth Pass

This walk follows almost the same route as the National Pass but is a little longer as the main section of the track picks its way through the forest at the base of the escarpment, rather than along the claystone edge above. The ladders down the side of the escarpment are fun (so long as you're not scared of heights) and the pool at the foot of the falls makes for good swimming.

At a glance

Grade: Hard

Time: 4 hours 30 minutes

Distance:
5.6 kilometre circuit (but feels like more!)

Ascent/Descent:
400 metres descent,
400 metres ascent

Weather: All conditions, but lovely and sheltered on a hot day

Closest public transport:
Local bus 685 runs past the corner of Fletcher St and Falls Rd, 500 metres from the picnic area

Finding the track

From Wentworth Falls railway station, turn right onto the Great Western Highway and then first left into Falls Road. Follow Falls Road for 1.7 kilometres to very end, and then follow signs to your right down to Wentworth Falls Picnic Area.

Walk directions

1 From the car park area, walk 300 metres along the tarred road to Wentworth Falls Lookout, where a large sign indicates the start of the Wentworth Falls Track.

2 Head downhill and turn right at the first fork, following signs to Wentworth Falls.

Rock pool, Jamison Creek

Walk 45 **Ladders and forests of Wentworth Pass**

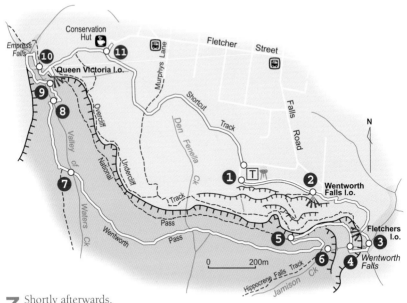

3 Shortly afterwards, turn left and continue straight ahead, following steps down to the top of the falls, where you cross on stepping stones. After a short level stretch, the track descends steeply down a series of old stone steps carved into the side of the cliff.

4 The track crosses back across Jamison Creek, immediately below the first drop of Wentworth Falls.

5 The track now zigzags westwards, hugging the base of the cliff. Keep your eyes out and after 200 metres or so, you'll see a track hairpinning back down to your left, signposted to Wentworth Pass via Slack Stairs. These stairs, consisting of nine sets of extremely steep ladders and topped off with a short scramble using a 2 metre handline are not for the faint-hearted. However, they are in fact quite safe and, with good adult supervision, okay for level-headed older children.

6 As the track meets the creek, you arrive at the base of the second drop of Wentworth Falls, where water cascades into a deep pool surrounded by a wide sandy beach. From here, continue on the main track staying on the right-hand side of the creek and following signs to Wentworth Pass. The track now continues along the base of the cliffline, passing through open forest of eucalypt and angophora, interspersed with moist pockets of tree ferns, lillipilli and sedges.

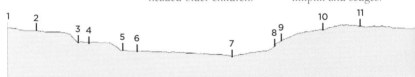

Walk 45 Ladders and forests of Wentworth Pass

Slacks Stairs

Slacks Stairs

Bridge on Wentworth Pass

7 After about 1.5 kilometres the track crosses three old iron footbridges and comes to a T-junction. (The track to the left goes to Vera Falls, see walk variations below.) Turn right, following the creek upstream.

8 A few minutes later, the main track crosses the creek again. There used to be a bridge here, but now you have to pick your way over the boulders. Sharp eyes will notice two blue metal markers nailed to boulders either side of the creek.

9 After about five minutes more walking uphill there's a T-junction with the National Pass. Head left, crossing the creek twice more (once at Lodore Falls, once at Empress Falls). The deep pools at Empress Falls are the last decent waterhole in the walk.

Walk variations

Where Wentworth Pass meets the bottom of the Valley of the Waters, you'll see a sidetrack marked to Vera Falls. See Walk 47 for more details of the Vera Falls section.

Walk 45 Ladders and forests of Wentworth Pass

10 At the next junction, fork to the right uphill, following signs to the Conservation Hut. Three sets of metal ladders lead up to Empress Lookout, followed shortly afterwards by Queen Victoria Lookout.

11 Just before the Conservation Hut finally appears on the horizon (although take a break here if you like), take the Shortcut Track leading off to your right. A level 20-minute walk takes you back to the Picnic Area where you started.

Currawong

Wentworth Falls

Mountains environment — Layers of time

Wentworth Falls is a good area to observe how the cliffs in the Blue Mountains are made up of several different layers. Looking at the falls themselves, you can see how the smooth vertical faces of the harder sandstone layers alternate with more easily eroded shale layers. Several of the tracks (such as the Overcliff Track, the Undercliff Track and the National Pass) make their way along shale ledges created by thousands of years of erosion. These ledges create a sheltered environment with swamps, overhangs and lots of shady spots to rest and admire the views.

Further down the mountains, the Hawkesbury sandstone isn't undermined by layers of shale in the same way, meaning that the sandstone doesn't break off in blocks but instead erodes in a way more reminiscent of coastal environments, with rounded boulders, caves and unusual shapes.

46 Hidden secrets of Roberts Pass

This historic track, built in 1903, follows a damp southern-facing gully between Inspiration Point and Moya Point, and makes for a slippery descent down mossy steps and rough ground, with a dramatic passage down a steep set of steps wedged inside a dark rock crevice. This walk earns its 'Hard' grading due to the poor condition of the track and the challenge in navigating.

At a glance

Grade: Hard

Time: 3 hours 15 minutes

Distance: 5.5 kilometre circuit

Ascent/Descent: 330 metres descent, 330 metres ascent

Weather: Avoid in heavy rain, great on a hot day

Closest public transport: Local bus 695 goes as far as Fitzroy St (weekdays only) - from here, it's 800 metres down to the resort car park

Finding the track

From Leura railway station, follow Railway Parade in an easterly direction. Take the seventh turn on your right (Gladstone Rd) and follow the street signs to the York Fairmont Resort. Head down to Level 4 of the resort car park.

Walk directions

1 On the eastern side of the car park, take the unsignposted track that leads across the edge of the golf course, heading past the tennis courts and through a wooded area. After 400 metres, next to the 14th tee, follow signs to Inspiration Point.

2 200 metres further along, turn right, again following signs to Inspiration Point.

The track can get very muddy!

Walk 46 **Hidden secrets of Roberts Pass**

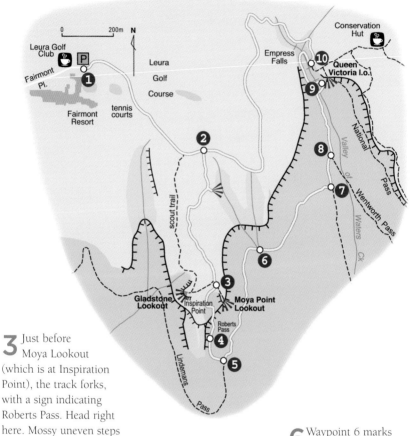

3 Just before Moya Lookout (which is at Inspiration Point), the track forks, with a sign indicating Roberts Pass. Head right here. Mossy uneven steps and dense leaf litter mark the way down this steep fern-filled gully.

4 Two flights of steps (one metal, one stone) plunge down a narrow crevice in the cliffline. (For many years, a single flat piece of iron lay where the metal steps are now, and walkers had to pull themselves up using a chain. These steps seem pretty luxurious in comparison.)

5 Two-thirds of the way down, a sign to the left points to the Valley of the Waters, with another sign pointing back up the way you came saying 'Roberts Pass Route Only'. You need to go left. The path gets boggy and indistinct along this section, but sticks to the base of the cliffs for most of the time. (Incidentally, the unsignposted track that continues south at waypoint 5 is the historic Lindeman Pass, described in more detail on page 146.)

6 Waypoint 6 marks where the track crosses a narrow gully, just below a small waterfall. If you're unsure about where the track goes at any point, look for white metal squares nailed to trees either side of the track.

7 Almost half a kilometre further on past the waterfall, you meet up with the Vera Falls track. Head left here, following signs to the Valley of the Waters.

8 After another 200 metres, the Vera Falls track meets up with Wentworth Pass (see Walk 46). Keep ascending straight ahead, following signs for the Valley of the Waters. You soon cross the creek over rounded boulders, continuing your steep climb.

9 Wentworth Pass meets up with the National Pass (see Walk 44) and the track bears left, crossing the creek once at Lodore Falls and then again at Empress Falls. Only a few minutes beyond Empress Falls, another track junction indicates the Nature Track straight ahead. This track leads down to a damp gully with a simple picnic bench. Continue on the Nature Track circuit to Lillian's Bridge.

10 Cross Lillian's Bridge, and continue up Lillian's Glen. Long stretches of boardwalks cross over delicate hanging swamp, with views peeking through to the Jamison Valley.

Narrow steps in the crevice of Roberts Pass

11 Only a kilometre past Lillian's Bridge, you arrive at the Inspiration Track turnoff (waypoint 2 on the map). Continue straight ahead to arrive at the resort car park where your walk began.

Walk variations

If you're feeling tired by the time you get to the Nature Track junction (waypoint 10), you can exit from the Valley of the Waters by walking up to the Conservation Hut. From here, catch a taxi back to where your walk began, or simply walk down Fletcher Street and along Falls Road back to Wentworth Falls Railway Station.

Roberts, Gladstone and Lindeman Passes

Lindeman Pass is an historic track built during the early 1900s which extends between Wentworth Falls and Katoomba along the base of the escarpment, with entry and exit points at Roberts Pass, Gladstone Pass and the Federal Pass. Construction and history of these passes is described in detail in local historian Jim Smith's (now out-of-print) *The Blue Mountains Mystery Track: Lindeman Pass*. Smith spent many weeks searching for the routes of these passes, clearing the tracks and 're-opening' Lindeman Pass (in an unofficial capacity) in 1984.

Out of the three passes, Roberts Pass is the only track that is maintained by National Parks. The other two passes don't appear on any current topographic maps and information about them is scarce. Both tracks present navigational difficulties: Lindeman Pass is very indistinct and confusing in places, and the steps leading down the side of Gladstone Pass are both slippery and highly exposed.

However, bushwalkers maintain a fascination with Lindeman Pass in particular, with the walk a regular on the schedule of most local bushwalking clubs. Keen overnight backpackers sometimes make a complete circuit of the Jamison Valley (Wentworth Falls to Katoomba via Lindeman Pass, Katoomba to Mount Solitary via the Federal Pass, then down Mount Solitary and up to Kings Tableland in Wentworth Falls via Kedumba Valley).

If you want to explore Lindeman Pass, try to go with someone who already knows the track. If this isn't possible, spend a few days getting familiar with the three main exits: Roberts Pass (see Walk 46, waypoint 5), the Federal Pass (see Walk 36, waypoint 7) and Gladstone Pass. You can find the entrance to Gladstone Pass behind the York Fairmont Resort, to the right of the potting sheds, where an old metal sign and intermittent ribbons on trees mark the steep south-facing descent down what is surely one of the Blue Mountain's most picturesque gullies. Try walking down Gladstone Pass, then east along a short section of Lindeman Pass, and then return full circle up Roberts Pass.

Lindeman Pass is still surprisingly easy to follow for most of its duration, with ribbons and faded metal markers marking the way. If at any point the track becomes like a bush-bash, and you have gone more than 100 metres without seeing a marker, turn around and head back to where the track was distinct. Then move ahead once more, looking carefully for markers. Take particular care to look for markers when crossing the large landslide.

Don't try to navigate Lindeman Pass alone. Go with at least two others, tell friends or the police where you're going, and try the walk in late spring or early autumn, when the days are longer. Remember that signals for both your GPS and your mobile phone are likely to be patchy at best, if not non-existent.

This partly overgrown and largely forgotten old walk wanders along the valley floor, following the creek until heading back up the Valley of the Waters. Sandstone stairs, waterfalls, leaf-covered tracks and a sense of solitude make for a challenging but inspiring day.

At a glance

Grade: Very Hard

Time: 6 hours

Distance: 7.3 km (but it feels like longer!)

Ascent/Descent:
650 metres descent,
650 metres ascent

Weather: All conditions, avoid in winter due to short days

Closest public transport: Local bus 685 runs past the corner of Fletcher St and Falls Rd, 500 metres from the picnic area

Finding the track

From Wentworth Falls railway station, turn right onto the Great Western Highway and then first left into Falls Road. Follow Falls Road for 1.7 kilometres to very end, and then follow signs to your right down to Wentworth Falls Picnic Area.

Walk directions

1 Follow the directions for Walk 45 (the Wentworth Pass), down Slacks Stairs and to the foot of Wentworth Falls (this is waypoint 6 on the map for that walk).

2 From the base of Wentworth Falls, continue along the main track as if you intend to continue along Wentworth Pass.

The sheltered fernery of the Hippocrene Track

Walk 47 Wentworth, Hippocrene and Vera Falls

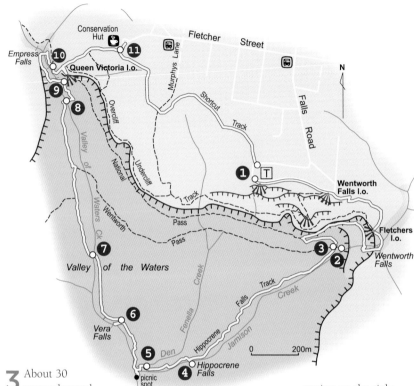

3 About 30 metres beyond the falls, you'll see a track leading down to your left (although there's no sign, the track is evidently well-established, with wide sandstone steps). This is the start of the Hippocrene Falls track. This narrow path steps down through sassafras, coachwood, lillipilli and turpentine, over mossy boulders and under huge turpentines. If you're in any doubt that you're on the right track, look out for the yellow blazes of paint and ribbon on the trees which appear about every 50 metres.

4 After a kilometre or so, you arrive at the sheltered Hippocrene Falls. From here keep following the track downstream, still staying on the right-hand side. The forest here is rather Tolkienesque with a thick canopy of tall trees overhead. The track becomes indistinct in places, with several confusing sidetracks, but keep looking for the square metal markers or coloured ribbons that mark the track from Hippocrene Falls onwards. If you walk more than 100 metres without

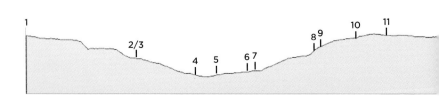

Mossy boulders on Jamison Creek

eeing one of these markers, ,o back until you do see ne and then look carefully o see where the main track eads.

5 Approximately 200 metres beyond Hippocrene Falls, the track moves away from Jamison Creek a little before crossing Den Fenella Creek. Shortly fter this crossing, an unmarked footpad on your eft leads to the junction of amison and Valley of Waters Creek. It's worth xploring this area; there's a reat picnic spot just on the

other side of Jamison Creek. From here, return to the main track and head upstream, on the right-hand side of the Valley of the Waters.

6 After only a couple of hundred metres an unmarked sidetrack leads down to the left. There are no yellow track blazes here, but a few ribbons mark this junction, next to a huge gum with fire-hollowed insides. Take the sidetrack down to the base of Vera Falls. A cave just to the right of the falls provides

shelter from the weather. After the falls, return to the main track and head steeply up the hill. The path becomes narrow, rocky and at times precipitous. Avoid the sidetrack leading down to the top of Vera Falls and stick to the right-hand side of the creek for another 300 metres or so.

7 You arrive at the creek once more. There are no signposts here (although you may spot the word 'OUT' painted on a nearby boulder) but cross the creek and keep heading uphill.

Picnic spot at Jamison Creek

The track is quite clear here. Ignore the sidetrack 500 metres further that leads left up to Roberts Pass and ignore the sidetrack shortly after that leads right down to Wentworth Pass.

8 The main track ascends quite steeply now, crossing the creek one more time at the base of Flat Rock Falls. There are no signs, but you may spot two blue metal markers on the rocks.

9 Shortly after crossing the creek, there's a T-junction with the National Pass. Head left uphill, crossing the creek twice more (once at Lodore Falls, once at Empress Falls). The deep pools at Empress Falls make for divine swimming and are the last decent waterhole in the walk.

10 At the next junction fork to the right uphill, following signs to the Conservation Hut.

Walk 47 Wentworth, Hippocrene and Vera Falls

Three sets of metal ladders lead up to Empress Lookout, followed shortly afterwards by Queen Victoria Lookout.

11 Just before the Conservation Hut finally appears on the horizon (although take a break here if you like), take the Shortcut Track leading off to your right. A level 20 minute walk takes you back to the Picnic Area where you started.

Vera Falls

Mountains history — Blue Mountains indigenous culture

In the Greater Blue Mountains, there are six indigenous language groups: the Dharawal in the south-east, the Gundungurra in the south, the Darug in the central east, the Wiradjuri in the central west, the Darkinjung in the north-east and the Wanaruah in the far north. Before European settlement, a number of routes were used by these different groups to travel across the Blue Mountains, to trade with one another, hunt for food or gather in ceremonies.

What we *do* know is that the process of colonisation was dramatic and brutal. Anywhere that Europeans settled, the Aboriginal people experienced dispossession of their land, a decline in food sources, the theft of essential tools and brutal killings. This direct impact was almost always followed by the spread of disease. Within one year of the British Fleet arriving in the Sydney region in 1788, one half of the local population had died of smallpox. By the early 1900s there were only a couple of small communities left in the Blue Mountains, living on the fringes of towns.

The resulting loss of knowledge regarding Blue Mountains indigenous culture is something that can never be completely recovered. However, the Aboriginal community *did* survive and slowly, through a combination of existing knowledge and archaeological exploration, a deeper understanding of Australia's cultural heritage is emerging. There are many hundreds of sites in the Blue Mountains and, if you spend much time in the bush in the Blue Mountains, you'll almost certainly come across a site of interest, such as a rock shelter, grinding grooves or engravings. Maybe you've passed these features many times before, but never realised how significant they are.

If you come across a site, be aware that this is part of our living history. For example, if you find a stone artefact, such as a flaked tool, leave it on the ground just where it was. Never touch pigment images, carve your name in a rock surface or shelter or attempt to enlarge grinding grooves. By respecting the significance of these sites, you are acknowledging Australia's indigenous history and its importance not just to the Aboriginal community, but to all Australians.

Adelina Falls

Lawson to Springwood

Elevation: From 732 metres (Lawson) to 371 metres (Springwood)

Population: 29,000

There are seven towns in the mid-mountains: Lawson, Hazelbrook, Woodford, Linden, Faulconbridge, Springwood and Winmalee. Out of these towns, Lawson and Hazelbrook retain that typical mountains feel with a fairly alternative community and lots of people who both live and work in the area. In contrast, Faulconbridge and Springwood are commuter-belt towns, with Springwood being the main shopping destination for people living in the mid-mountains.

Walks 49 and 50 are a long way from the nearest bus or train station, so double-check you can receive mobile phone reception at the walk's end if you decide to rely upon a taxi. Walk 54 is kilometres away from the nearest bus stop.

PUBLIC TRANSPORT

Walks 48, 51, 52 and 53 are easy if you're relying on public transport as they start and finish relatively close to train stations. Walks 49, 50 and 53 are a long way from the nearest bus or train and even calling a taxi can be difficult as mobile phone reception is patchy at the end of both of these walks.

Little Terrace Falls

48 Picnics on Waterfall Circuit

This local favourite starts from the industrial area in South Lawson. The vegetation is lush and varied, with woodlands of Sydney peppermints, bloodwood and angophoras interspersed with patches of coachwoods, black wattle and ferns. On a hot summer's day, you can spend a slow afternoon wandering from waterfall to waterfall (there are four within the space of three kilometres), enjoying the shade, beach areas and peaceful surrounds. This walk is on Council reserve, so dogs are permitted.

Finding the track

From Lawson railway station, cross the highway (there's a subway if you're on foot). Head down Honour Avenue for one kilometre. A sign indicates the start of the track, immediately opposite Livingstone Street.

Walk directions

1 Head off down the well-made track. After only 150 metres, you come to a crossroads, with a fire trail cutting across the track. Keep going straight ahead. Descend timber steps past a fenced lookout of Adelina Falls and down to Lawson Creek.

At a glance

Grade: Easy

Time: 1 hour 30 minutes

Distance:
3 kilometre circuit

Ascent/Descent:
125 metres descent,
125 metres ascent

Weather: All conditions

Closest public transport:
Lawson railway station,
1 km away

Cataract Falls

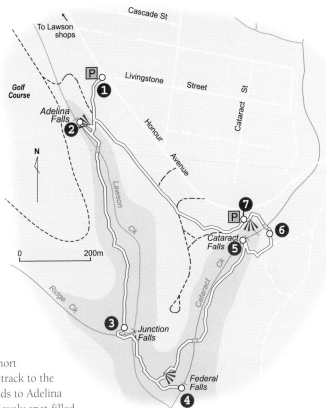

2 A short sidetrack to the right leads to Adelina Falls, a lovely spot filled with ferns. The shallow water makes a perfect paddling spot for children. Back on the main track, the route soon crosses to the right-hand bank of the creek.

3 600 metres further on, the track bends around to your right (ignore the faint track leading off to your left), ducks under a ledge, crosses Ridge Creek and then zigzags down to where a footbridge crosses Lawson Creek. Either side of the footbridge, short sidetracks lead to the twin falls of Junction Falls. From here, it's only another 200 metres until a set of stone steps branch off to the left. Note these steps, but continue straight ahead.

4 You soon arrive at Federal Falls, where a barbecue fireplace (check current fire restrictions first), a big beach and lots of shade make for an ideal picnic spot. From here, return to the stone steps, turning right and ascending steeply to a fenced lookout (with views over Cataract Creek) and head north-east along Cataract Creek, crossing to the right-hand bank.

Walk 48 Picnics on Waterfall Circuit

5 Just as the track starts to leave the creek, a short sidetrack leads to the shady Cataract Falls, where a large overhang makes a cool resting spot on a hot day. The area downstream of here used to be known as Shakespeare Glen in the early 1900s. From here, return to the main track, which ascends from the gully on a series of stone and timber steps.

6 At the top of the steps, turn left along the fire trail for about 50 metres and then take the track signposted Lawson which branches off to your left, crossing Cataract Creek on a wooden footbridge. This track leads past a couple of old unsignposted lookouts and emerges at a picnic area just off Honour Avenue.

7 Follow the fire trail that runs parallel to Honour Avenue for 500 metres before joining up with the track you left an hour or so earlier. Turn right and continue up the hill for another 150 metres until arriving back at the start point. (Alternatively, if you're with children, one of the adults can run ahead and bring the car back to the picnic area, as this fire trail can be hot and tiresome in summer.)

Angophora

Junction Falls

Walk variation

For a summer's night expedition with a bit of a difference, set off from the bottom car park on Honour Avenue (waypoint 7) and pick your way down to Cataract Falls (waypoint 5). Switch off your torch, stand quietly under the shelter recess next to Cataract Falls and let your eyes adjust to the light. Before long, you'll see how the walls of this recess are covered in glow-worms whose bioluminescence shines like stars in the night sky.

49 Dreamy beauty of Terrace Falls

To leave the dusty fire trails of Hazelbrook and step down into the rainforest gullies of Terrace Falls is always a surprise. Fern-filled crevices, hidden waterfalls and quiet pools make this cool, shady walk seem like another world, and the difficult access (you need a 4 wheel drive to navigate the fire trails), make it surprisingly private.

At a glance

Grade: Medium

Time: 2 hours

Distance: 4.4 kilometre circuit, including sidetracks

Ascent/Descent: 140 metres descent, 140 metres ascent

Weather: All conditions, but offers lots of shade in hot weather

Closest public transport: Hazelbrook railway station, 3.8 km away

Finding the track

From Hazelbrook railway station, head east along Railway Parade and take the second road on your right (Valley Road). Head down Valley Road for 2 kilometres until a fire trail branches off to your right, signposted to Terrace Falls Walking Track.

Walk directions

1 From the Terrace Falls sign, descend the rough firetrail until you come to a picnic area. Keep going straight ahead. After 200 metres you'll see a clearing on your left. Leave the firetrail here, following signs to Terrace Falls Walking Track. The track descends gently towards the creek, passing huge sphinx-like boulders known locally as 'The Pyramids'. Halfway down, two tall mountain grey gums frame either side of the track.

Terrace Falls

Walk 49 Dreamy beauty of Terrace Falls

2 As the track bends sharply to the right at the creek line, take the short sidetrack to your left that leads to Pyramid Falls. The water here comes from a catchment that many years ago housed the delicately-named 'nightsoil depot'. (Not a great spot to refill your water bottles.) From here, return to the main track and continue your gradual descent.

3 You soon arrive at Bedford Creek, where signs indicate left to Bedford Pool, and right to Terrace Falls. Turn left. After 40 metres, you arrive at Bedford Pool (also known as 'The Lake'). After resting at the pool, cross on stepping stones and look for a slightly overgrown track that heads up the hill from the far (southwest) corner.

4 After 200 metres the track leads down to Lester Pool, a natural

waterhole that few people visit. From here, return to where the main track met Bedford Creek and this time go straight ahead, following signs to Terrace Falls. The track is level and ducks under long rock shelters, including one with a seat hewn out of stone.

5 As the main track veers north, a sign indicates the Willawong Pool sidetrack on your left. Take this sidetrack, which crosses the creek almost immediately.

6 Shortly after the crossing, keep your eyes peeled for an old mossy fireplace on the left-hand side. Immediately opposite this fireplace, the Old Western Track zigzags up the hill, offering an overgrown and adventurous alternative route to Terrace Falls. However, for this walk, ignore the Old Western Track and keep going straight ahead. This sidetrack to Willawong Pool only takes ten minutes or so but is truly lovely, winding under long pockmarked overhangs, fire-blackened

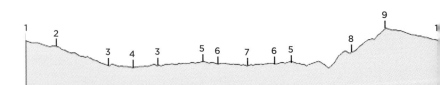

Old sign (pre-1949)

Bedford Creek

by periods of Aboriginal occupation.

7 At Willawong Pool, where Lawson Creek meets Bedford Creek, there's a secluded camping spot, surrounded by rainforest vegetation. After resting here, return to the main track, turning left when you reach it. From here, follow signs to Terrace Falls. You soon cross the creek twice, first at Little Terrace Falls, next at Salote Pool.

8 Past a long rock overhang, a sidetrack leads down to the dreamy Terrace Falls, where cascades tumble down twelve broad, shallow terraces. It's fun to clamber up the cascades, rockhopping from one level to another, but do watch your step as it's very slippery. When you're ready, return to the main track. A series of stone steps (originally constructed in 1892) ascend from the gully.

9 At the T-junction halfway up the hill, turn right, following the sign to Car Park 2. You soon arrive at a car parking area. Turn left and walk for 100 metres up to a T-junction. Turn right and follow this firetrail back to the first car park (waypoint 2), and then back, past the picnic area and up to Valley Road where the walk began.

For families

On a rainy day, Selwood Science and Puzzles, located just over the railway bridge at Hazelbrook, is a great place to spend a couple of hours. A mixture between a gift shop and an educational centre, the weatherboard cottage includes a room devoted to puzzles and jigsaws, a room full of quiz books and science books, and a science lab packed with different kits and toys for kids and enthusiasts (including all the dinosaur kits that budding palaeontologists could ever long for). Selwood Science also runs kids activity workshops during the school hols. For more info, visit www.selwoodscience.com.au or phone 4758 6235.

50 Martins Lookout to Lost World

With two steep descents and two steep ascents, this walk is ideal for those on a fitness mission. The track is poorly signposted and overgrown in places, so take care and allow an hour or so extra the first time you do this walk. Glenbrook Creek is the midway point on both the outwards and the return journey and makes the perfect spot for languid picnics and skinny-dipping.

Finding the track

Head east from Springwood Railway Station along Macquarie Street for 1.2 kilometres and take the third road on right (Burns Road). Go along Burns Road for 1 kilometre and turn left into Farm Road. After 600 metres, take the right-hand fork at Batman Park and continue along the dirt for another 2 kilometres until you arrive at Martins Lookout car park.

Walk directions

1 Head down from the car park area. After a few metres, ignore the sidetrack that branches off to the right. This is the Short Track, a rough, steep route that heads down to Glenbrook Creek and joins up with the Sassafras Gully circuit (see Walk 52).

At a glance

Grade: Hard

Time: 4 hours

Distance:
6.3 kilometres return

Ascent/Descent:
465 metres descent,
465 metres ascent

Weather: Avoid in really hot weather

Closest public transport: Local bus 693 goes as far as the corner of Burns Rd and Lalor Rd, 2.5 km away

Glenbrook Creek

Walk 50 **Martins Lookout to Lost World**

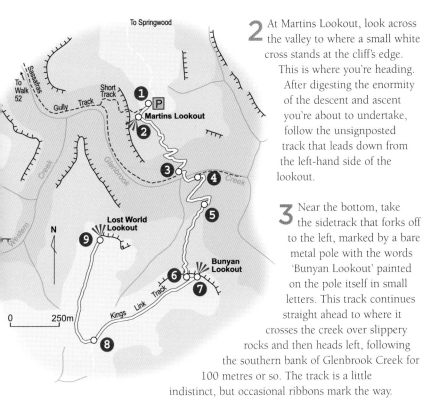

2 At Martins Lookout, look across the valley to where a small white cross stands at the cliff's edge. This is where you're heading. After digesting the enormity of the descent and ascent you're about to undertake, follow the unsignposted track that leads down from the left-hand side of the lookout.

3 Near the bottom, take the sidetrack that forks off to the left, marked by a bare metal pole with the words 'Bunyan Lookout' painted on the pole itself in small letters. This track continues straight ahead to where it crosses the creek over slippery rocks and then heads left, following the southern bank of Glenbrook Creek for 100 metres or so. The track is a little indistinct, but occasional ribbons mark the way.

4 At an unsignposted fork in the track bear right. Only a couple of metres further on, there's an old metal pole with the words 'Kings Link' painted on it. From here, the ascent is along a narrow but distinct track, with stone steps winding steeply upwards.

5 About halfway up, a rocky outcrop offers filtered views over the valley. From here, continue your ascent along the nose of the ridge for another 300 metres.

6 You emerge through a gap between two boulders at the escarpment's edge, next to a tree marked with a white blaze. Make a mental note of this spot so you don't get lost on your return journey. Bear left.

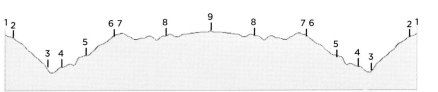

View from Martins Lookout

7 Bunyan Lookout is another 50 metres further on, an exposed crag with views back down to Glenbrook Creek. From here, an easy sandy track leads southwest for 650 metres.

8 At a small green sign that points to 'The Lost World', turn right.

9 Lost World Lookout is quickly reached, marked by a white cross which was erected to honour the memory of Reverend Raymer. The Reverend led many bushwalks in the area and died in Wollongong in 1953 attempting to rescue a pupil from the sea. After enjoying this bird's-eye view, return to Martins Lookout the way you came.

Link Track at sunset

Walk variations

At Glenbrook Creek, leave the track and explore downstream, where you'll find a series of wide swimming holes with water of a blue so deep it's almost turquoise. For those feeling curious, on the northern bank downstream from the creek crossing, there's a vertical rock face on which someone has chiselled the 23rd Psalm.

Glenbrook Creek

Mountains environment — Water quality

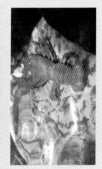

Blue Mountains City Council, together with volunteers from the Living Streams Streamwatch program, regularly monitor the health of Blue Mountains waterways. Water quality is generally good and many creeks support a healthy range of macro-invertebrates such as juvenile insects, crustaceans (freshwater crayfish and shrimp), leeches and freshwater snails. However, there are still significant challenges facing the waterways, including sedimentation, leaks from sewerage lines and pollution from stormwater.

In towns with larger populations such as Springwood and Katoomba, significant percentages of the catchment areas are covered in impervious surfaces such as bitumen and concrete, forever changing the way that water moves through the environment. When rain falls on these surfaces it cannot soak through — instead it runs off and is quickly transported to drainage lines and creeks, carrying with it pollutants and moving at damaging speeds. Nowadays, many of the creeks run almost dry for most of the year but burst their banks after heavy rain, a distinctly different pattern from the steady supply of water that used to flow along these creeks in times gone by.

Sedimentation is another major problem. Although stringent conditions are applied to development applications, best practice often falls by the wayside and sediment can come from any area of bare dirt. A good example of sedimentation is at Minnehaha Falls in North Katoomba. The plunge pool at the base of the waterfall was once known as 'bottomless' and was measured at over 90 feet deep. Today the pool is knee deep at most because it is full of sand from development and erosion in the catchment. Another waterway badly affected by sedimentation is Govetts Creek in North Leura, which is filling up with sand and silt washed by rain from recent roadworks on the highway.

51 Bellbirds at Sassafras Gully

This is not only one of the best walks in the Lower Mountains, it's also one of the quietest. You start from Faulconbridge railway station and follow Sassafras Creek through eucalypts and rainforest all the way to where the Wiggins Track branches off, heading back up to Springwood. From there, it's an easy walk back through the streets to Springwood station.

Finding the track

If you're driving, park at the commuter car park on the northern side of Faulconbridge station and walk across the overpass to the southern side. If you're travelling by train, get off at Faulconbridge Station and turn left across the overpass. Walk parallel to the railway in an easterly direction (with the railway tracks on your left). The route starts on the right-hand side of No. 10 Sir Henrys Parade, just after the road bends around to the right.

Walk directions

1 Zigzag down behind the houses through open woodland, ignoring the faint track that veers off to the left after a few minutes. The muddy trickle that is the headwaters of Sassafras Creek is soon crossed, first to the right bank, then back to the left bank. You arrive at a cool mossy spot where a small waterfall drops through boulders and tall turpentines create a thick canopy overhead.

At a glance

Grade: Medium

Time: 3 hours, plus train travel time

Distance: 6.6 kilometres one way

Ascent/descent: 260 metres descent, 195 metres ascent

Weather: Suitable for all conditions, beautiful after light rain

Closest public transport: The track starts 350 metres from Faulconbridge railway station and finishes at Springwood railway station

Sassafras Creek

Walk 51 Bellbirds at Sassafras Gully

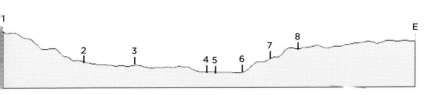

2 Past some dry eucalypt woodland, there's a rocky outcrop where burnt signs on a tree point to Clarinda Falls and Sassafras Creek. After a short descent, take the short sidetrack on your left to Clarinda Falls. A sign indicates that the water isn't safe to drink. That's fine, but the dark stain's behind Clarida Falls are caused by iron in the water, not pollution.

3 Half a kilometre further on, Numantia Creek comes in from the right. There's a small clearing and fireplace here, a nice spot. The vegetation gets more jungly from this point onwards, with lots of vines, cedar wattles and lilli pilli.

4 As the track approaches closer to the creek, look for the crossing that hops over rocks to the left bank,

currently marked by strands of coloured ribbon (if you find the track running out and ending up in the creek, then you've missed this crossing!)

5 Shortly after the crossing there's a track junction. To the left, Sassafras Gully provides an early exit (see Walk 53). But to continue, cross the sidecreek and head southwards, downstream on the left-hand bank of Sassafras Creek, crossing after 350 metres.

6 Three-quarters of a kilometre from Sassafras Gully turnoff, a sign points ahead to Perch Ponds. Take the unsignposted track to the left that crosses Sassafras Creek on a wooden footbridge. A minute or so later, where a (mostly dry) creek comes in from the right, look for a sign pointing uphill to the Wiggins Track. Follow mossy old stone steps as they ascend steeply up the left-hand side of the gully.

Walk 51 Bellbirds at Sassafras Gully

Make sure to keep zigzagging steadily upwards — if the track starts to get rough, then you've missed a bend. The honeycomb whirled shapes in the Hawkesbury sandstone cliffs are reminiscent of Sydney terrain.

7 Two-thirds of the way up, a rather grand metal and timber bridge spans what is now a tiny trickle. In spring, the new bark of angophoras shines almost luminous salmon pink.

8 Just a little further on, the track finishes at the end of Yondell Avenue. Turn left and follow Yondell to where it meets Bee Farm Road. Follow Bee Farm to the end, turn right into Valley Road and left into Homedale Street. Finally, turn right onto Macquarie Road and walk up to Springwood railway station.

Sassafras Creek

Mountains environment — Iron staining

Sometimes you may come across creeks where partially submerged boulders and surrounding rock faces are almost orange in colour. Your first impression is probably that the water is highly polluted. However, this colour is more commonly caused by bacteria that oxidises the iron present in the water (many rocks and soils in the Blue Mountains are naturally high in iron) and is a completely natural phenomenon. Even more off-putting is the oily film you may see on top of the water. This film isn't oil at all, but again is associated with iron bacteria.

Nonetheless, regardless of where you are in the Blue Mountains, you're best to avoid drinking from the creeks, even if they do give the appearance of being pristine. This practice is particularly important especially after heavy rain, when pollutants are often carried down into the waterways.

Walk variations

If you're feeling energetic, wander up Numantia Creek as far as Numantia Falls (the creek comes in at waypoint 3 on the map). There's a faint footpad that goes along the left-hand bank, crossing to the right-hand bank shortly before the falls themselves. In the 1930s, Sir Martin built a track that led from his house 'Numantia' right down to the falls, and in some places, remnants of old sandstone steps can still be found.

Victory Track

52 Creek circuit on Wiggins Track

This circuit combines the beginning of Walk 53, leading down Sassafras Gully and along Sassafras Creek for some distance before joining up with the end of Walk 51, which follows the Wiggins Track back up to Springwood.

Walk directions

1 Follow the directions for Walk 53 as far as waypoint 5. This is where the Wiggins Track connects with the Sassafras Gully walk.

2 Follow the directions for Walk 51, starting at waypoint 6 and going as far as waypoint 8.

3 At waypoint 8, either follow the directions as per Walk 51 to return to Springwood railway station or alternatively, if you left your car at Sassafras Gully Road, go left into Valley Road at the end of Bee Farm Road and then left into Sassafras Gully Road.

At a glance

Grade: Medium

Time:
2 hours 30 minutes

Distance: 4.8 kilometre circuit

Ascent/descent:
170 metres descent,
180 metres ascent

Weather: Suitable for all conditions

Closest public transport:
The walk starts 1.2 km from Springwood Railway Station and finishes at Springwood Railway Station.

Lichen covered tree

53 Swimming holes on Glenbrook Creek

Down in the gullies only minutes from neat-as-a-pin suburbia, shady footpaths meander through a rainforest fairyland, leading down to swimming holes at the junction of Glenbrook and Sassafras Creeks, before winding back up to the town along Magdala Creek. This walk starts and finishes close to public transport.

At a glance

Grade: Hard

Distance: 8.9 kilometre circuit

Time: 4 hours

Ascent/descent: 250 metres descent, 235 metres ascent

Weather: Suitable for all conditions, great summer swimming

Closest public transport: The walk starts 1.2 km from Springwood railway station and finishes 200 metres from Springwood railway station

Finding the track

From Springwood station, turn right along Macquarie Road (where all the shops are). Go past the Fire Station and turn first left into Homedale Street. Then turn right into Valley Road, ignoring signs to Sassafras Gully, cross over Bee Farm Road (again ignoring signs) and keep going until you see Sassafras Gully Road on your left. The track starts 180 metres further down, at the end of this road.

Walk directions

1 The track descends gently, the open woodland of banksia, acacia and dillwynia soon changing into sheltered rainforest. A small gully opens up to your right. Look up at the swirling sandstone patterns as you pass under an overhang.

Swimming hole at the junction of Sassafras and Glenbrook Creek

Walk 53 Swimming holes on Glenbrook Creek

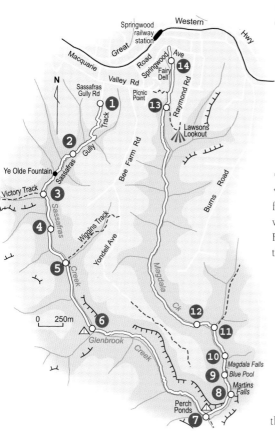

2 Cross the creek on the bedrock and continue downstream on the right bank. After five minutes or so, you pass an overhang where a natural spring spurts from a crevice between two boulders. A faded sign reads 'Ye Olde Fountain'.

3 Sassafras Creek cuts in from the right about five minutes further on. This is where the Victory Track from Faulconbridge joins up. Ignore this track and keep going straight ahead, across the creek. You're now heading downstream on the left-hand bank of Sassafras Creek, damp ferns brushing against your legs.

4 A sign to Sassafras Gully Reserve indicates where you cross the creek on stepping stones.

5 700 metres from the Victory Track turnoff, an unsignposted track branches off to the left. This is where the Wiggins Track leads back up to Bee Farm Road. Ignore this turnoff and continue straight ahead.

6 700 metres further along, there's a large clearing and camping area where Sassafras Creek meets Glenbrook Creek, the best swimming hole of the entire walk. From the clearing, keep to the left, cross Sassafras Creek and continue downstream on the left-hand bank, of Glenbrook Creek winding through a leafy undergrowth of sassafras and fragrant mint bushes with tall turpentines overhead. Further on, occasional footpads head down to summer beach spots.

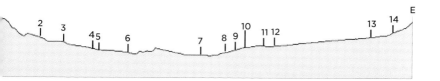

Sassafras Junction

7 After 1.5 kilometres, there's another clearing and camping area. This is Perch Ponds, a series of shallow but very pretty pools. From here, follow the signs up to Magdala Gully, leaving Glenbrook Creek behind and heading northwards.

8 Five minutes further on, you come to Martins Falls on your right. A sidetrack leads around under the falls to the deep, wide pool below. This is the last possible swimming hole for this walk.

9 After another 200 metres there's a sign to Magdala Falls. A short sidetrack leads to an unfenced outcrop that looks down to the jade waters of the Blue Pool below. The surrounding cliff walls make this pool virtually inaccessible.

10 Continuing upstream, watch out for where the track crosses to the right-hand bank of the creek five minutes further on. Although unsignposted, you know you're at the right spot if you can see where the creek plummets down through a hole worn into the bedrock at the point where you cross.

11 300 metres after the creek crossing, just beyond a series of rust-gold-brown overhangs, there is a clear fork in the track. Straight ahead is an old (very rough in places) track that leads up to the back of Burns Road. Ignore this track and instead turn sharp left, crossing the sidecreek.

12 Shortly afterwards, just as the track draws close to the water, cross to the left-hand bank of Magdala Creek. This crossing is easy to miss, but arrows carved in the bedrock show the way. From here, continue along Magdala Creek, crossing the creek several times. In dry weather, the water is scarcely more than a trickle here, but during heavy rain these creek crossings can be tricky to navigate.

13 At a junction the track up to your right leads to Lawsons Lookout, but you need to head left following signs to Springwood. Only a couple of minutes later, a footbridge marks another junction. Here, keep straight ahead following signs to the fern-carpeted Fairy Dell.

14 The track emerges next to the old scout hall and some picnic tables, from where a bitumen road leads up to Springwood Avenue, at the walk's end.

Reflections at Perch Ponds

For families — Baby carriers

If you have a child under two years old and you want to go bushwalking, then spend the money and invest in a quality baby carrier. For new babies, a front pouch works best, but after a few months, you'll find that carrying your child on your back is the only way to go. Macpac are probably the most reputable range (available from specialist outdoor equipment stores), and although the price tag starts at a hefty $249, they'll last through a few children (all depends how keen you are!). Macpac also offer carrier attachments such as the 'Sleepyhead' (for your babe to rest their neck when they fall asleep) and the 'Sombrero' (a canopy arrangement that offers protection from sun, wind and rain).

54 Birdwatching at Blue Gum Swamp

Only a few minutes away from the bustling shopping centre of Winmalee, this surprisingly lovely valley is home to one of the last stands of Blue Gum Forest in the lower Blue Mountains, with a sidetrack half way along that culminates in a lookout over the Grose River. A favourite among birdwatchers, over 122 species of birds have been recorded at Blue Gum Swamp, with up to 49 species in a single day.

Finding the track

From Winmalee Shopping Centre, head north along Whitecross Road for 1 kilometre. The track starts at the end of Whitecross Road, next to a NPWS information sign and gate.

At a glance

Grade: Medium/Hard

Time: 5 hours

Distance: 13 km (or 9 km circuit only)

Ascent/Descent: 270 metres descent, 270 metres ascent

Weather: Autumn, winter and spring

Closest public transport: Bus 692 goes to Winmalee Shopping Centre, 1 km away

Walk directions

1 Head downhill along a clear firetrail that runs behind the houses.

2 After a few minutes, there's a clear firetrail junction. The route described here goes clockwise, but you can also walk this circuit anti-clockwise. (The section between waypoints 8 and 10 can be exposed and hot, so if you're walking this track on a summer's morning, you're best to go anti-clockwise.)

3 Note the tall Deanes Blue Gum, with its blue-grey bark peeling back to expose a creamy skin underneath, 25 metres or so before a NPWS locked gate. The valley floor either side of the muddy waters of Blue Gum Swamp Creek is dominated by these Blue Gums, which grow up to 50 metres high on the deep, alluvial soil. Birdsong fills the valley in the early mornings, with brown thornbills, fan-tailed cuckoos, honeyeaters, king parrots, kookaburras and lorikeets amongst the most frequently-spotted species.

4 If you walk along this firetrail in the evenings, you may well spot swamp wallabies, greater gliders or yellow-bellied gliders. NPWS often run night spotting trips during school holidays; phone 4787 8877 for details.

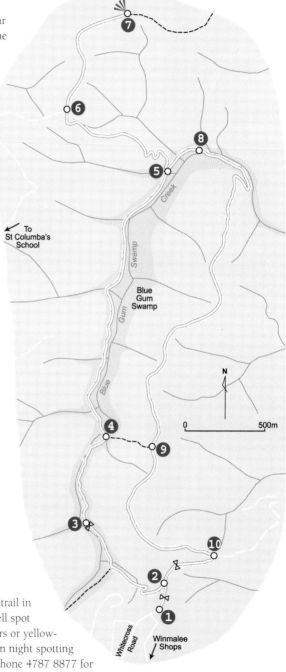

Walk 54 Birdwatching at Blue Gum Swamp

5 Almost three kilometres from the NPWS gate, you come to another track junction. Turn left, following signs to Bees Nest Hill and Grose Head South. (Or, if you're feeling tired, you can continue straight ahead around the circuit, cutting four kilometres off the walk.) The energetic ascent up Bees Nest Hill marks a change of vegetation communities, with the prickly, exposed vegetation typical to Hawkesbury Sandstone.

6 At the next firetrail junction, head right, following signs to Grose Head South. (The trail that goes left leads to private land at the back of St Columba's College.)

7 At the firetrail's end, a rocky unfenced lookout offers view to North Grose Head opposite, with the junction of Springwood Creek and the Grose River way below. If you're feeling adventurous, a footpad follows the ridge from the lookout for another 30 minutes or so, arriving at the trig point at the top of South Grose Head (also called Grose Mountain). Be careful if you decide to explore here, as the track goes very close to the edge of precipitous cliffs. Otherwise, after enjoying the views

from the lookout, return down Bees Nest Hill to waypoint 5, and turn left.

8 A picnic area with barbecue fireplace provides a sheltered spot for resting or birdwatching. From here, the firetrail ascends sharply to Shaws Ridge. This ridge can make for uncomfortably hot walking in summer, but at other times of year the wildflowers provide ample reward, especially in late winter and spring.

9 A couple of kilometres further on, painted arrows mark where the shortcut track exits due east from waypoint 4.

10 Follow the main trail as it bends sharply around to the right, ignoring the sandy firetrail that branches off to the left. Shortly beyond a locked gate, you arrive at the first track junction (waypoint 2). From here, turn left back up to the car park area.

Walking track at Blue Gum Swamp

Walk variations

About a third of the way north along the Blue Gum Swamp Track (800 metres after the NPWS gate), a concrete slab and some random rocks mark a shortcut across to Shaws Ridge. This narrow track is clearly marked with white paint and involves a short easy scramble near the beginning. If you then return south along Shaws Ridge, this creates a shorter circuit of about four kilometres.

Warrimoo to Glenbrook

Elevation: From 270 metres (Warrimoo) to 163 metres (Glenbrook)

Population: 14,600

The Lower Mountains do not have the same wonderful selection of historic tracks and canyon-like views that you find in the Upper Mountains. However, the warmer climate of the Glenbrook area not only makes for ideal winter bushwalks (you can leave Katoomba when it's five degrees and find yourself basking behind a sunny rock in Glenbrook only an hour or two later), but also lends itself to wonderfully lazy summer bushwalks, when you stagger a kilometre or two down to a swimming hole, relax for a few hours and then wend your way back home.

Unlike anywhere else in the Blue Mountains National Park, the entrance at Glenbrook not only has a gate that is locked every night, but cars have to pay a fee of $7 to enter. The gate is locked at 7pm during daylight saving and at 6pm the rest of the year, and re-opens at 8.30am. (If you get stuck on the wrong side of the gates after hours, you can phone 131 911 and someone will let you out, but a fee does apply.)

You may find that the gates at Glenbrook are locked on occasions, even during regular opening hours, as the causeway is prone to flooding (phone 4787 8877 to check if you're not sure).

PUBLIC TRANSPORT

Although a couple of the walks in this chapter both start and finish at train stations, several of the walks in Glenbrook National Park are impossible to reach by public transport and require either a car or a push bike. However, you may want to take a taxi as far as the park gates. Blaxland Glenbrook Taxi Service. T 4739 4888.

55 Bird's-eye view from Nepean Lookout

A wide sandy fire trail leads to a lookout with views down to the Nepean River and Erskine Creek. This is one of the few walks in the Lower Mountains that you can do with a stroller (so long as it's a decent one that can survive a few bumps), but do be careful with children as the lookout itself is unfenced.

Finding the track

Heading east from Glenbrook railway station, follow Burfitt Parade and then Bruce Road for 1.2 kilometres until you arrive at the NPWS entrance gates. From here, continue straight ahead along The Oaks Fire Trail for 8 kilometres. Shortly after The Oaks Picnic Area, the road forks to the left, with signs to Nepean Lookout. Continue for another 4 kilometres until you arrive at Nepean Lookout car park.

At a glance

Grade: Easy

Time: 40 minutes

Distance:
1.4 kilometres return

Ascent/descent: 40 metres descent, 40 metres ascent

Weather: Avoid in hot sun

Closest public transport:
Glenbrook railway station, 13.3 km away

The broad waters of the Nepean

Walk 55 Bird's-eye view from Nepean Lookout

Walk directions

1 The fire trail leads down from the car park. In the late afternoon, you may see the occasional wallaby bound across the track.

2 At the end of the trail, Nepean Lookout is a large (unfenced) outcrop of sandstone, with a sheer drop down to the Nepean River. Around to your right, another lookout provides glimpses of where the Nepean joins with the clear waters of Erskine Creek.

3 Return the way you came.

By Nepean Lookout

For families — Judging how far your child can walk

If you haven't done much bushwalking before, you may be wondering just how much your children are capable of doing. Is it realistic to ask a five-year-old to walk seven kilometres? Is your teenager going to be okay on a two-day hike?

There's no right or wrong answer. Almost any child will walk all day long if they're used to it and are well supplied with yummy food and drink (over the years, the author's three children have road-tested almost every walk in this book). The trick is to build up slowly, starting with easy walks and figuring out what's comfortable and what your kids enjoy. Also, with younger children, remember to allow more time than the suggested times in this book. That way you'll have time to hang out and play, and not have to spend all day driving the kids along at a pace that makes everyone miserable.

Scribbly gum

Black ash

Sydney peppermint

Scribbly close-up

Mountains environment — Identifying gum trees

One of the reasons that the Blue Mountains is listed as a World Heritage Area is the wide representation of eucalypt habitats in the region, with at least 92 species occurring in the Greater Blue Mountains Region.

Unless you're a horticulturist, learning to tell the differences between eucalypts is tricky. However, in the open forest on the ridge tops (which forms the backdrop to all the Blue Mountains towns), there are some trees that are easily identifiable. The Sydney Peppermint (*Eucalyptus piperita*) is the most common tree in the Blue Mountains. Its bark is dark grey and fibrous at the base but sheds in ribbons from the upper branches, exposing smooth, pale white limbs. The Black Ash (*Eucalyptus sieberi*) is another dominant species, usually found growing alongside the Sydney Peppermint. Its bark is a darker grey and more deeply furrowed, with shiny red new branchlets. The Scribbly Gum (*Eucalyptus sclerophylla*) is another common eucalypt, a slightly smaller tree with a contorted habit. The bark is silvery grey and often covered in scribbles caused by the burrowing of insect larvae.

56 Kangaroos at Euroka

Euroka is a great place to take overseas visitors for a picnic, as you're almost guaranteed to see kangaroos. The site of an ancient volcanic vent formed at least 150 million years ago, these days Euroka is a small valley with fertile soil and grassy clearings. This track makes a circuit that starts and finishes at Euroka, visiting the Nepean River along the way.

Finding the track

Heading east from Glenbrook railway station, follow Burfitt Parade and then Bruce Road for 1.2 kilometres until you arrive at the NPWS entrance gates. Go down the hill, over the causeway, and along The Oaks Fire Trail to the first intersection, 1.5 kilometres away. Turn left, following signs to Euroka. At Euroka, there's a T-junction at the bottom of the hill. Turn left following signs to Darug camping area, from where the track begins.

At a glance

Grade: Easy

Time: 1 hour 30 minutes

Distance:
3.2 kilometres circuit

Ascent/descent:
135 metres descent,
135 metres ascent

Weather: Avoid in hot weather, ideal in spring and autumn

Closest public transport: Glenbrook railway station, 5.5 kilometres away

Walk directions

1 Head straight ahead across Darug camping area following signs to Nepean River. The clearing on your right is a great place to see Grey Kangaroos, particularly at dawn or dusk. These kangaroos were introduced to Euroka in 1968 and have thrived ever since.

Grey Kangaroos at dusk

Walk 56 **Kangaroos at Euroka**

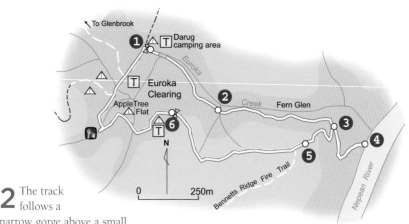

2 The track follows a narrow gorge above a small creek, where the enclosed walls on either side create a microclimate in which coachwoods, lilly pillies and tall eucalypts flourish. Look for hollowed out trees created by bushfire. Such trees are prized shelter for many different animals.

3 Almost a kilometre from the camping area,

Waratah in full bloom

the track forks. A short descent down to your left leads to the Nepean River.

4 The Nepean runs broad and quiet, a deep brown-green colour. Like many wide rivers, the swimming isn't that safe here, and if you have young children they're best to paddle in the adjacent sidecreek. When you're ready, head back up to the junction (waypoint 3). At the junction, turn left, following signs to Euroka via Bennetts Ridge.

5 You emerge at a fire trail turning circle. Follow this trail until it meets up with Bennetts Ridge fire trail, and then turn right. This area is

particularly striking in late winter when acacias flower everywhere. The bush is so quiet that it's hard to believe that Sydney is only a few kilometres away.

6 A short descent leads you back down to Euroka. Follow the road around to where a creek comes in from your left, just past Apple Tree Campsite. If you explore the rock platforms around here, you'll find several set of grinding grooves (Euroka was a camping ground for Aboriginal people for many thousands of years). From here, the road winds back towards Darug camping area where the walk began.

Nepean River

Out and about — Camping at Euroka

Limited numbers, abundant grassy clear areas and lots of wildlife make Euroka one of the best spots for camping in the Blue Mountains. Facilities include compost toilets, picnic tables, wood barbecues and rubbish bins. You're best to bring your own drinking water (you can fill up from a tap near the park entrance).

There are five camping areas, each of which is suitable for up to 20 people: Appletree Flat, Bennetts Ridge, Daruk, Nioka and Redgum. You can choose between camping areas where you park your car close to your tent, or quieter camping areas where cars are parked a little further away.

Although NPWS provide limited firewood for barbecues, check in advance regarding fire restrictions, as you won't be able to make a fire if there's high fire danger. If you're in any doubt, bring your own gas/fuel stove.

The rates are $5.00 per adult or $3.00 per child per night, as well as a $7 vehicle day pass for each day you stay. The main entrance gate is locked at 7pm during daylight saving or at 6pm during the rest of the year, and re-opens at 8.30am.

To book, phone the NPWS Richmond Office (T 4588 5247). If possible, try to book at least two weeks in advance, especially in peak times such as long weekends and school holidays.

Although this is a relatively short walk, the track is rather tricky between Glenbrook Gorge and Jellybean Pool. You're best to allow heaps of time for rock-hopping and discovering the nooks and crannies of Glenbrook Creek. The deep swimming hole at Jellybean Pool makes a great reward for your efforts before you set off back up the hill.

Finding the track

Heading east from Glenbrook railway station, follow Burfitt Parade and then Bruce Road for 1.2 kilometres until you arrive at the NPWS entrance gates. At the far end of the car park, beyond the visitor centre, a service road leads down to your left. The Gorge Track starts just before a gate as this road curves to the left.

Walk directions

1 At the top of the track, a NPWS sign declares that the Gorge Track takes four hours return. Don't sweat — it only takes this long if you go all the way to the Nepean River and back (which you're not about to do). Timber steps descend a steep slope dotted with huge sandstone boulders, Sydney peppermints, grass trees and in early summer, clusters of fragile flannel flowers.

At a glance

Grade: Medium/Hard

Time: 1 hour 30 minutes

Distance:
2 kilometre circuit

Ascent/descent:
100 metres descent,
100 metres ascent

Weather: Suitable for all conditions, great in summer

Closest public transport:
Glenbrook railway station,
1.3 km away

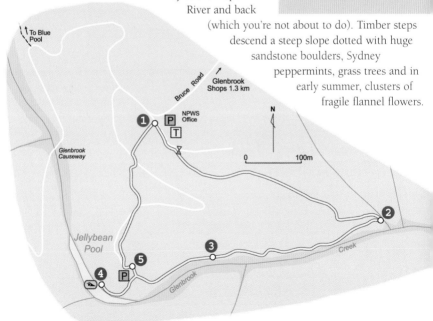

2 Approaching Glenbrook creek, a timber footbridge crosses a small inlet. Don't cross this bridge but turn hard to your right.

3 Most of the way, there's a rough footpad running parallel above Glenbrook creek on the right-hand side although sometimes the track disappears altogether. However, in summer, it's more fun to stay next to the creek and take your time rock-hopping from boulder to boulder, exploring shallow pools and pockmarked rock platforms.

4 After 400 metres, you arrive at the sea-green Jellybean Pool, a favourite local swimming area. Don't dive from the rocks here, as submerged boulders lie just below what look like deceptively deep pools.

Jellybean Pool

5 After enjoying Jellybean Pool, take the steps that lead straight up from the Pool to the car park just above. From here, follow the steps that shortcut across the zigzagging road, directly up to the NPWS car park where you began.

Mountains environment

In many of the Lower Mountains walks, you'll see wombat scats (otherwise known as wombat poo) in conspicuous spots along the track. Wombat scats have a distinctive cube-like shape, usually deposited in clusters of four to eight pellets. You usually see wombat scats on a log close to where the animal has been feeding, next to burrows or on tracks leading to burrows.

Every wombat's scats have a different smell and are one of the ways wombats communicate with each other. For example, scats help a wombat find its own burrow when it returns after a busy night looking for food and also tell other wombats if a burrow is occupied.

58 Yabbies and picnics at Crayfish Pool

Ample shade, a sandy beach, picture-postcard waterfalls and a wide swimming hole make for a languid place to while away a summer's afternoon. The track is uneven and rough, with boulders and indistinct arrows marking the descent.

Finding the track

Heading east from Glenbrook railway station, follow Burfitt Parade and then Bruce Road for 1.2 kilometres until you arrive at the NPWS entrance gates. From here, continue straight ahead along The Oaks Fire Trail for about 8 kilometres until you see Red Hands Fire Trail branching off to your right (just past The Oaks Picnic Area). Turn right here, but pause to look at your odometer. Drive another 3.9 kilometres until you see an unsignposted car park area on the right-hand side of the road. The walk (also unsignposted) starts directly opposite.

At a glance

Grade: Medium/Hard

Time: 1 hour 10 minutes (plus time for swimming)

Distance: 1.8 kilometres return

Ascent/descent: 110 metres descent, 110 metres ascent

Weather: Suitable for all conditions

Closest public transport: Glenbrook railway station, 13 km away

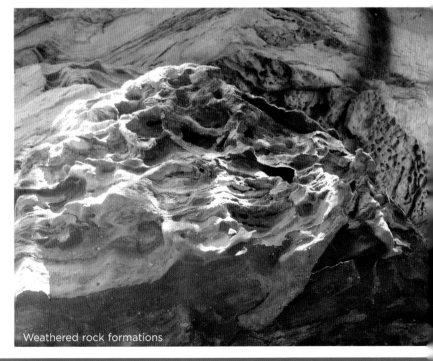
Weathered rock formations

Walk 58 Yabbies and picnics at Crayfish Pool

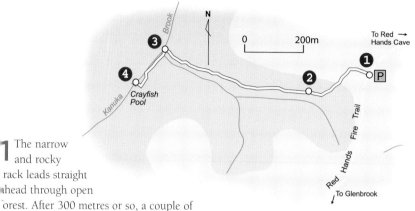

1 The narrow and rocky track leads straight ahead through open forest. After 300 metres or so, a couple of faint sidetracks lead off to the left. Ignore these and continue straight ahead following occasional arrows pointed or scratched into rocks. The track descends gradually but stays well above the gully that runs parallel on your left.

2 Be observant as you descend. There are no signs, save for the occasional arrow scratched or painted onto the rocks, and you don't want to get confused on your return journey. The ground drops away steeply at some points, with one or two short scrambles. (However, if you find yourself bushbashing then you know you've lost the main track and you need to go back and look for it.)

3 After about 20 minutes you arrive at Kanuka Brook. Turn left. The track becomes a little indistinct but runs close to the creek, underneath some fine overhangs, before dropping down into Crayfish Pool. This is a great spot, with a waterfall, shade, yabbies, sandy beach and a wide swimming hole. Apparently, you can climb up the waterfall to explore further upstream, but this would be a difficult scramble requiring rope.

4 After enjoying the waterfall, return the way you came.

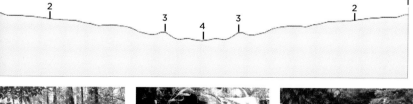

Track leading down

A short scramble

Crayfish Pool

59 Winter sun on Jack Evans Track

This has to be one of the loveliest short walks in the lower Blue Mountains. Starting near Nepean Lookout, this track zigzags down to the clear waters of Erskine Creek. On a sunny day, there's nothing better than taking a picnic and a good book and spending the day snoozing on the riverbanks and cooling off in swimming holes.

Finding the track

Heading east from Glenbrook railway station, follow Burfitt Parade and then Bruce Road for 1.2 kilometres until you arrive at the NPWS entrance gates. From here, continue straight ahead along The Oaks Fire Trail for 8 kilometres. Shortly after The Oaks Picnic Area, the road forks to the left, with signs to Nepean Lookout. Continue for another 4 kilometres until you arrive at Nepean Lookout car park.

At a glance

Grade: Medium

Time: 1 hour 30 minutes

Distance:
2.5 kilometres return

Ascent/descent:
190 metres descent,
190 metres ascent

Weather:
Sublime in sunny weather

Closest public transport:
Glenbrook railway station,
13.3 km away

Walk directions

1 The track starts at the back left-hand corner of the car park, marked by a huge sign which states that this track is graded 'Hard' and takes four hours return. Don't be discouraged: only a few metres further on another sign states the track takes two hours return, which is a much fairer estimate.

Cascades on Erskine Creek

Walk 59 **Winter sun on Jack Evans Track**

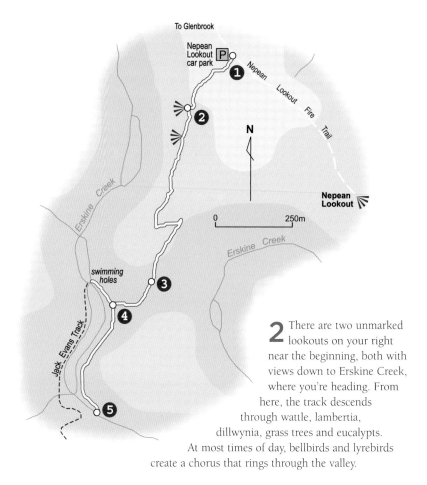

2 There are two unmarked lookouts on your right near the beginning, both with views down to Erskine Creek, where you're heading. From here, the track descends through wattle, lambertia, dillwynia, grass trees and eucalypts. At most times of day, bellbirds and lyrebirds create a chorus that rings through the valley.

3 After about 15 minutes descent, you arrive at a saddle between two peaks. A faint sidetrack on the left-hand side at this saddle leads down to the Nepean.

4 Just before the creek, the track forks at an unsignposted junction. The best swimming holes and beach area are down to your right, only 100 metres further along. In 1945, a dam-worker by the name of Jack Evans blazed a track that continued from this spot along the other side of Erskine Creek, leading all the way to Warragamba Dam. Most of this track now passes through Water Board restricted zones. You can spend an idyllic day rock-hopping along Erskine Creek in either direction. Platypuses have been sighted here (the best times to spot platypus are at dawn and dusk).

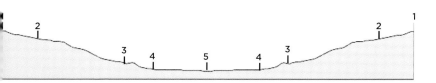

Swimming holes at Erskine Creek

5 Alternatively, head left rather than right at the junction. About 300 metres downstream this leads to another lovely swimming area, where massive boulders almost dam the creek where it bends around.

Euroka track

60 Rock art at Red Hands Cave

This easy circuit takes you through along the Link Track down to a shady spot on Campfire Creek, and then winds up along the banks of a narrow creek to arrive at Red Hands Cave, where an overhang protects a wall covered with hand paintings.

Finding the track

Heading east from Glenbrook railway station, follow Burfitt Parade and then Bruce Road for 1.2 kilometres until you arrive at the NPWS entrance gates. From here, continue straight ahead along The Oaks Fire Trail for about 8 kilometres until you see Red Hands Fire Trail branching off to your right (just past The Oaks Picnic Area). Drive to the end of this road to the car park area.

At a glance

Grade: Easy

Time: 2 hours

Distance: 4 km circuit

Ascent/descent: 120 metres descent, 120 metres ascent

Weather: Perfect in spring and autumn

Closest public transport: Glenbrook railway station, 13.5 km away

Walk directions

1 Look for the signposted Link Track that descends on a gradual grade through an open woodland of eucalypts. (For a detailed map of this circuit, refer to waypoints 5 to 9 on the map for Walk 61.)

2 The track meets up with Campfire Creek, a narrow creek lined with dense foliage on either side.

3 A little further on, where a sidecreek comes in on the right-hand side, look carefully at the rock bed of the creek, where there are several sets of grinding grooves.

4 400 metres further on, the track forks. Keep to the left, following signs to Red Hands Cave.

5 Near the head of the creek is Red Hands Cave, one of the most significant rock art sites in the Blue Mountains region. Despite the perspex viewing screen, this remains a special place. From here, it's a short ascent up to the car park where the walk began.

Mountains history – Red Hands Cave

Red Hands Cave is one of the most significant examples of rock art in the Lower Mountains, featuring a panel of artwork with up to 70 hand stencils. Aboriginal people created these hand stencils by spraying ochre from their mouths over a hand pressed on the rock's surface. Red ochre was the most commonly used pigment, but you'll also see both white and yellow hand stencils in other areas of the mountains.

Rock art specialists debate the meaning of these stencils and what they represent. Hand stencils are about connection with country and moving through country, probably following the idea of the part representing the whole, a kind of signature recording the visit to the site. In other parts of Australia, children would sometimes leave a stencil with their left hand as part of an early initiation ceremony, and then would return to the same site as adults to leave a stencil of their right hand.

Red Hands Cave also includes a banana-shaped figure and four balloon-shaped outlines in red ochre. The four balloon motifs are interesting in that this same shape appears in other areas in the Blue Mountains, and again, there are differences of opinion as to what this shape represents. This is a good example of why rock art shouldn't be considered in isolation but needs to be placed in the context of a total landscape. Related rock art features, oral history, contemporary Aboriginal perspectives and layers of meaning are all important aspects to consider.

Contemporary Aboriginal artists use motifs from rock art as inspiration for their own artworks. This process exemplifies how Aboriginal culture is not something frozen in time that archaeologists struggle to interpret, rather it is a culture that is as dynamic as it is diverse.

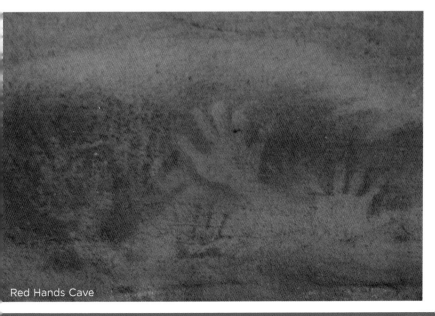

Red Hands Cave

61 Camp Fire Creek to Red Hands Cave

This walk takes you through a pretty gully all the way to Red Hands Cave, one of the most significant examples of rock art in the Blue Mountains. Despite the distance, the track is fairly level, making it an ideal walk for those who want to stretch their legs and get some exercise, but don't want to slog up the side of a cliff at the end of the day.

At a glance

Grade: Medium

Time: 4 hours

Distance:
9.2 kilometres circuit

Ascent/descent:
300 metres descent,
300 metres ascent

Weather: Perfect in winter, avoid in summer

Closest public transport:
Glenbrook railway station,
1.3 km away

Finding the track

Heading east from Glenbrook railway station, follow Burfitt Parade and then Bruce Road for 1.2 kilometres until you arrive at the NPWS entrance gates. The track starts here. (You can drive your car another 500 metres down to the Blue Pool car park area, but there's a $7 entrance fee.)

Walk directions

1 From the NPWS car park, follow the bitumen road downhill until you arrive at the causeway. Cross to the other side.

2 Look for the sign that indicates the start of the Red Hands Cave walk, just to the right of the causeway. This track follows the left-hand bank of Camp Fire Creek. At almost any time of year you'll see a variety of flowering native plants along this sheltered gully, many of which acted as food sources for Aboriginal people.

Grinding grooves on Camp Fire Creek

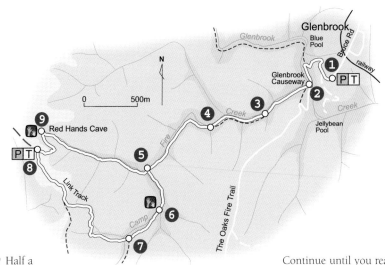

3 Half a kilometre further on, the track forks. This junction is unsignposted and easy to miss when you're heading in this direction, so you may end up on the lower track that runs right next to the creek, or on the higher track that runs parallel. (The lower track has a little more shade and is probably better in summer.)

4 600 metres further on, the two tracks meet again at a footbridge that traverses a sidecreek. Cross the footbridge over the sidecreek and continue your journey along the left-hand bank of Camp Fire Creek.

5 Before long, bear left at another junction, following signs to the Link Track. Follow Camp Fire Creek for another 400 metres.

6 A trickle of water comes in from your left and there's a NPWS interpretative sign next to the track. Right here on a rock platform in the middle of the creek you'll find several sets of grinding grooves. You may even find flakes left from tool making under the overhangs in the surrounding areas.

Continue until you reach a sign indicating where the Link Track branches off away from the creek.

7 Cross Camp Fire Creek and head up the hill. (The old Camp Fire Creek circuit used to take a slightly different route here, but was largely destroyed in the Christmas 2001 bushfires.) See if you can spot the woody pear shrubs along here. The distinctive fruit looks just like a wooden pear and can be up to 9 cm long.

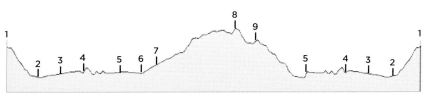

Walk 61 Camp Fire Creek to Red Hands Cave

Distinctive weathering patterns

8 The track pops out at Red Hands Cave car park area, where there's a toilet and barbecue grill. From here, a sign indicates where the Red Hands Cave track circles back.

9 A short descent takes you down to Red Hands Cave. The iron mesh and perspex viewing screen may seem overkill, but before this protection was put into place the cave wall was subjected to several incidents of vandalism. Once your eyes adjust to the light, you should be able to see many sets of overlapping hand stencils as well as a distinctive balloon-shaped motif. Continue following the track as it runs along the right-hand side of what is mostly a dry creek until you arrive back at waypoint 5 on the map. From here, return the way you came, back up to the NPWS car park.

62 Secrets of Florabella Pass

One of the prettiest walks in all of the Lower Mountains, this track winds along Florabella Creek and then Glenbrook Creek. Wildflowers, shelter caves, swimming holes, interesting sidetracks and lots of shady spots to rest make this a great adventure at any time of year.

Finding the track

The track starts on the southern side of Warrimoo railway station.

Walk directions

1 From the railway station, cross the highway on the overpass. Turn right, following the service road that runs parallel to the Great Western Highway, past Warrimoo shops, until you come to The Boulevarde on your left. At the end of The Boulevarde, turn right into Arthur Street and then first left into Florabella Street.

2 The walking track itself starts at the end of Florabella Street, descending steeply past wind-hollowed sandstone walls and over wide sandstone steps towards Florabella Creek. Further down, open forest and tall, pink angophoras merge into a grove of lilly pillies as the track follows the left-hand bank of the (often dry) creek.

At a glance

Grade: Medium

Time: 3 hours 30 minutes

Distance:
6.2 kilometres one way

Ascent/descent:
330 metres descent,
280 metres ascent

Weather:
Suitable for all conditions

Closest public transport:
The walks starts at Warrimoo railway station and finishes at Blaxland railway station

Flannel flowers

Walk 62 Secrets of Florabella Pass

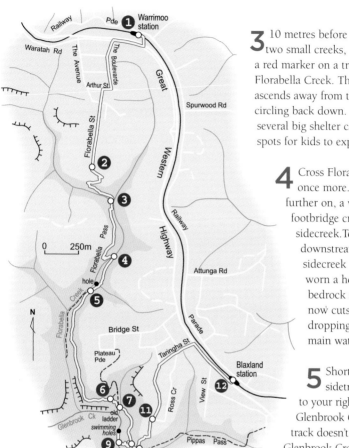

3 10 metres before a meeting of two small creeks, look for a red marker on a tree, and cross Florabella Creek. The track then ascends away from the creek before circling back down. As you descend, several big shelter caves make fun spots for kids to explore.

4 Cross Florabella Creek once more. 200 metres further on, a wooden footbridge crosses a sidecreek. Ten metres downstream on this sidecreek the water has worn a hole in the bedrock so deep that it now cuts right through, dropping down to the main watercourse below.

5 Shortly afterwards, a sidetrack leads down to your right, signposted to Glenbrook Creek. (This track doesn't actually go to Glenbrook Creek, but ends at a pleasant spot on Florabella Creek.) Ignore this sidetrack and keep going straight ahead, continuing for another kilometre along a level stretch. The steep gorge to Florabella Creek falls away on your right-hand side; flannel flowers bloom all the way along in early spring. Way below out of sight, Florabella Creek meets up with Glenbrook Creek.

6 You arrive at a fork. You need to bear right, past a sign that says 'Exit via Ross Crescent', winding down towards the creek. (If you bear left, an old track, signposted to Plateau Parade, goes under a large overhang (ideal for picnics) and continues straight ahead, past a small grotto and up some old stone steps, emerging at the back of Bridge Road in Blaxland.)

7 100 metres or so from the track junction, a sidecreek comes in from your left. If you go right here, you can make a rather perilous but very direct descent down slippery rocks and an old ladder to Glenbrook Creek. Instead, go straight ahead, crossing the sidecreek and continuing south, quite high above the left-hand bank of Glenbrook Creek.

8 Follow this rocky, rather precipitous track for about 250 metres, watching out for a faded sign painted in white saying 'Warrimoo Blaxland' on a large brown-black rock on the left-hand side. Just here, take the unsignposted sidetrack that hairpins sharply to your right, descending to the creek. This route is very steep and has exposed steps cut into boulders. (Keep a careful eye on any children if you decide to do this part of the walk.)

9 You soon arrive at Glenbrook Creek, where there's a string of excellent swimming holes. If you explore a little further upstream, you can see the spot where the ladder descends down the side of a small waterfall into a crescent-shaped gully. Once you've finished exploring, head back up the hill to the main track. Turn right.

10 Almost immediately, a sign nailed to a tree indicates 'Exit Via Ross Crescent'. Follow the steps up for a short, relatively steep ascent. The track forks near the top. Keep right and ascend steps between large boulders.

11 At the top, a short section of dirt track emerges onto Ross Crescent, between numbers 56 and 58. From here, make your way along Ross Crescent and then Taringha Street up to the Great Western Highway. From here, turn right, heading towards Blaxland shops.

12 From Blaxland railway station, catch the train to wherever you need to go.

Hollowed cave

Creek bed, Florabella Creek

Walk 62 Secrets of Florabella Pass

Walk variations

Instead of exiting via Ross Crescent at waypoint 10, you can follow the sheltered and rather lovely Pippa's Pass to where it emerges behind Blaxland library. (If you're doing this walk in reverse, the track starts in the south-western corner of the car park, next to a timber gate with a Private Property sign.)

Grass trees on Florabella

63 Off-track adventure along Glenbrook Creek

Although not the longest walk in this book, the nature of the terrain makes this one of the most challenging. Despite being shown on local maps, this track is indistinct, overgrown and at times seemingly non-existent. Nonetheless, deep swimming holes, tranquil surroundings and a true sense of being off the beaten track make this a great day out for the intrepid bushwalker.

Finding the track

The track starts on the southern side of Blaxland railway station.

Walk directions

1 From the station, cross the overpass to the shops and turn right, following the Great Western Highway. After 400 metres, turn left into Taringha Street and then left into Ross Crescent.

2 Between numbers 56 and 58 Ross Crescent, a sign saying Florabella Pass marks the beginning of a track that leads down behind the houses. At the end of the houses, two green metal posts (with the sign they once held long since burnt) mark the beginning of Florabella Pass itself. Keep to the left, following steps as they lead down between large boulders. At the foot of the steps, turn right at the T-junction.

At a glance

Grade: Very Hard

Time: 7 hours

Distance:
9.5 kilometres one way

Ascent/descent:
160 metres descent,
70 metres ascent

Weather:
Avoid in mid-summer

Closest public transport:
The walk starts at Blaxland railway station and finishes at Glenbrook railway station.

Rock shelves alongside Glenbrook Creek

Walk 63 Off-track adventure along Glenbrook Creek

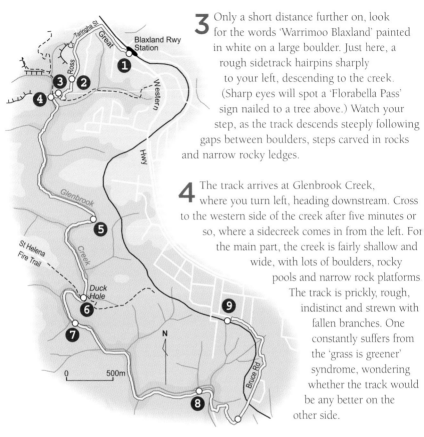

3 Only a short distance further on, look for the words 'Warrimoo Blaxland' painted in white on a large boulder. Just here, a rough sidetrack hairpins sharply to your left, descending to the creek. (Sharp eyes will spot a 'Florabella Pass' sign nailed to a tree above.) Watch your step, as the track descends steeply following gaps between boulders, steps carved in rocks and narrow rocky ledges.

4 The track arrives at Glenbrook Creek, where you turn left, heading downstream. Cross to the western side of the creek after five minutes or so, where a sidecreek comes in from the left. For the main part, the creek is fairly shallow and wide, with lots of boulders, rocky pools and narrow rock platforms. The track is prickly, rough, indistinct and strewn with fallen branches. One constantly suffers from the 'grass is greener' syndrome, wondering whether the track would be any better on the other side.

5 After 1.75 kilometres, Glenbrook Creek bends sharply to the right creating broad sandy river flats. The track goes along the creek bed for a short distance before continuing. Things get a little easier after this, with less lawyer vine and more clearly defined footpads.

6 Another kilometre further on leads to Duck Hole, a natural waterhole that used to be a water source for steam engines. On the western side, a very rough route leads up to St Helena's fire trail. On the eastern side, an alternative exit leads up the right-hand side of the gully and connects with a network of fire trails. Unfortunately, this track now ends up at the railway lines, meaning an illegal crossing of the railway tracks for any who decide to return to Glenbrook this way. The track crosses to the left-hand side a minute or so beyond Duck Hole.

Walk 63 **Off-track adventure along Glenbrook Creek**

Morning light and winter wattle on Glenbrook Creek

7 Continue following Glenbrook Creek downstream, crossing to the right-hand bank at a wide pool 500 metres further on.

8 It's another fairly slow 2 kilometres to Blue Pool, a 200 metre-long swimming hole that gets its colour from the way sunlight refracts through clay particles suspended in the water. You can cross Blue Pool at either end — a rough track exists on both sides. From the far end Blue Pool, a clear path leads up to the road and then up to the NPWS car park at the top.

9 An easy walk along Bruce Road and then Burfitt Parade takes you to Glenbrook railway station and a well-earned rest.

Carlotta Arch, Jenolan Caves

Exploring Further Afield

Bushwalkers visiting the Blue Mountains usually spend most of their time exploring the ridge between Wentworth Falls and Katoomba. However, the Blue Mountains is a huge area, and there are many walks to the north along the Bells Line of Road, to the west around Lithgow, and southwest towards Jenolan Caves and Kanangra Walls.

The basalt soil along the Bells Line of Road nourishes spectacular wildflower displays in spring at Mount Banks, and also the many display gardens at the picture-perfect village of Mount Wilson. Behind Mount Wilson lies an intricate network of deep canyons, one of which is described in Walk 65.

Further west, still in canyon country, the Newnes Plateau is a different kind of landscape yet again. Walk 64 explores the incandescent Glow Worm Tunnel and the ancient pagoda rock formations that surround it.

To the southwest, only an hour's drive from Blackheath, lies Jenolan Caves, and a short distance beyond that, Kanangra Walls. Make a weekend of it, spending time exploring the bush around Jenolan Caves as well as the magnificent caverns beneath. And nothing beats driving out to the 'edge of the wilderness' at Kanangra Walls to watch the early morning on the sheer sandstone cliffs, with Kanangra Gorge five hundred metres below.

Jenolan River waterfall

64 Glowworms, canyons and railways

Abandoned railway lines, pagoda-shaped rock formations and old coach roads lead to an ideal picnic destination at Newnes River ford. A historic track circles back past valley views, under tall fern canopies and finally, through a dark tunnel filled with thousands of glittering glow worms. Remember to wear strong footwear and to take a torch.

Finding the track

From Bells Line of Road (also known as Chifley Road at this point), turn left into Newnes Forest Road at the Zig Zag railway turnoff. Head right, cross the railway tracks, and keep right as you head up the hill. After 8.8 km, turn right at the T-junction with Glowworm Tunnel Road. Continue straight ahead for another 26.9 km to the Glowworm Tunnel car park. This route follows dirt roads and isn't suitable for 2wd vehicles with low clearance. Alternative access is via Newnes: from Wallerawang, follow Wolgan Road for approximately 27 km until the road crosses a weir (waypoint 5 on the map), and park here.

At a glance

Grade: Medium

Time: 5 hours

Distance: 10.5 kilometres return

Ascent/descent: 350 metres descent, 350 metres ascent

Weather: All seasons

Closest public transport: None

The Old Coach Road

Walk directions

1 From the car park, a clear track heads past metal barriers and along the old railway embankment, following signs to the Glowworm Tunnel. Built in 1906 to haul oil shale from the mines at Newnes up to Clarence, this railway ran for over 50 kilometres, passing through two tunnels (of which the Glowworm Tunnel is one) and dropping almost 700m at a steep gradient.

2 100 metres or so beyond a small footbridge is an intersection. Head right here, following signs for the Pagoda Track to Old Coach Road. Massive cone-shaped sandstone outcrops (known as pagodas) shape the skyline.

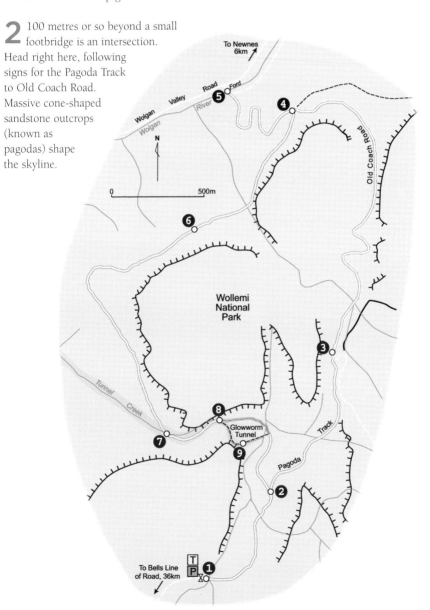

3 A kilometre or so further on, the track meets up with the Old Coach Road firetrail. Go straight ahead, following signs to Wolgan Valley Junction. Formerly the main road into Newnes, this quiet firetrail leads through tall stands of grey gums, with views to Wolgan Valley in the east.

Exploring the Glowworm Tunnel

4 At a distinct track junction, a walking track heads right to Newnes (through private property). To the left, the circuit continues. Straight ahead, an optional diversion descends steeply to the old ford on Newnes River, passing the old colliery. This ford makes for a lovely picnic spot, but adds another 1.5 kilometres and 70 metres descent/ascent to your trip.

5 The ford provides an alternative starting and finishing point for this walk, accessible from Wolgan Road. It's also a very pleasant (albeit unofficial) camping spot. From here, ascend back up the hill to waypoint 4 on the map and turn right.

Walk variations

A shorter version of this walk is to skip the Pagoda Track and instead go direct to the Glowworm Tunnel. At the far end of the tunnel, either return the way you came or head to your left and follow the rough track through Bell's Grotto Canyon back to the beginning of the tunnel. From here, return to the car park the way you came. The circuit takes approximately an hour and a half and is about 3 kilometres long.

6 You're now walking along the old railway line once more, with tall sandstone walls marking the way (the line was built in just 13 months, quite a feat of engineering and determination). Views open up to Donkey Mountain as the track curves south.

7 As the cliff walls get closer together and the temperature begins to drop, you enter a mini-canyon environment filled with tall ferns.

8 Finally, you arrive at the Glowworm Tunnel. Walk slowly, keep your voice to a whisper, and use your torch as little as possible. You'll be rewarded by the velvet black of the tunnel transforming to a starlit sky with celestial patterns of glow worms. Stick to the left-hand side and your feet probably won't get too wet.

9 When you exit the tunnel, the track continues straight ahead for about 300 metres until you're back at the Pagoda Track junction (waymark 2 on the map). However, if you're still full of energy, double-back to your right immediately after the tunnel to explore Bells Grotto Canyon. When the railway was in use and the weather was fine, passengers walked through Bell's Grotto to avoid the black smoke and fumes from the tunnel.

10 From waypoint 2, make your way back along the Glowworm Tunnel Track to the car park.

Out and about – Exploring the Lithgow area

The historic mining town of Lithgow provides a great base for exploring the Wollemi National Park, which includes Deep Pass Canyon, the beautiful Wolgan Valley, historic Glen Davis and the surrounding Capertee Valley (which boasts more birds per square kilometre than anywhere else in the Southern hemisphere). Or for a step back in time, visit the Great Zig Zag Railway and take a steam train journey through Blue Mountains scenery filled with sights, sounds and smells of a bygone era.

The Great Zig Zag Railway

This bushwalk takes you to the beginning of one of the most popular canyons in the Blue Mountains. Although this route doesn't take you down the canyon itself (a trip only for the fit and well-prepared), you can get a taste of the canyon environment by spending a couple of hours exploring the slow running waters of Wollangambe Creek. Take your swimmers, a picnic and good non-slip shoes (Dunlop Volleys are good when climbing over slippery rocks and fallen trees in the creek itself).

Finding the track

The track starts at the Bushfire Station on The Avenue at Mount Wilson. (There are toilets and parking here, but no drinking water.)

At a glance

Grade: Hard

Time: 3 hours, but allow extra for exploring

Distance: 6.3 km (plus side-trips) return

Ascent/Descent: 300 metres descent, 300 metres ascent

Weather: Best in summer

Closest public transport: None

Views on the descent to Wollangambe

Walk 65 Canyons at Wollangambe

Walk directions

1 The Wollangambe Track starts behind the bushfire station, leading northeast (parallel to the road) for 200 metres.

2 At the T-junction, turn left. Descend straight ahead along this firetrail for 500 metres.

3 The firetrail meets a T-junction with another firetrail, but look closely and you'll see a rough track straight ahead, signposted as the Wollangambe River Track (this is the last sign you'll see — the rest of the track is unsignposted). The vegetation changes here, with lots of tea-tree, geebung and silvery-white scribbly gums scraping out an existence in tough sandy soils.

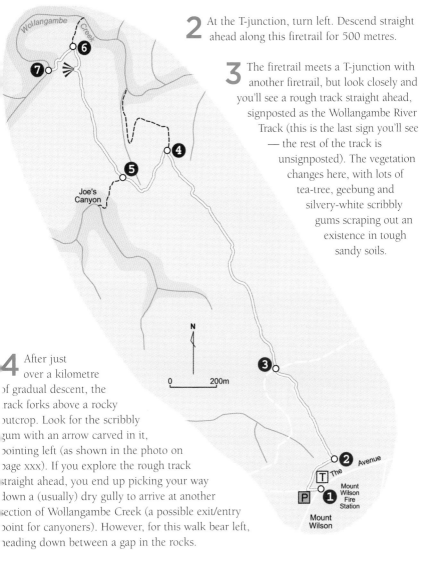

4 After just over a kilometre of gradual descent, the track forks above a rocky outcrop. Look for the scribbly gum with an arrow carved in it, pointing left (as shown in the photo on page xxx). If you explore the rough track straight ahead, you end up picking your way down a (usually) dry gully to arrive at another section of Wollangambe Creek (a possible exit/entry point for canyoners). However, for this walk bear left, heading down between a gap in the rocks.

5 After 300 metres, ignore the sidetrack that bears off to the left from a narrow saddle and keep straight ahead. (However, if you feel inquisitive, head down here for 200 metres to take a peek at one of the many narrow side creeks in this area. This route is the beginning of Joe's Canyon, an easy half-day canyon that follows Du Faur Creek and Bell Creek down to the Wollangambe.)

Walk 64 Canyons at Wollangambe

Walk variations — exploring Mount Wilson

There are many other walks in Mount Wilson, lovingly documented in a booklet called *Mount Wilson Walks*, by Elizabeth Raines. Take the time to explore the lush environment of the Cathedral of Ferns circuit, or the dripping rainforest of the Waterfalls Walk, both short walks that start from the picnic ground.

6 600 metres further on, just after an opening on the left with dramatic views over Wollangambe and Bell Creek, the track bends sharply to the left. (Another track also bears to the right at this point, heading north, down to an alternate spot on the Wollangambe with good swimming holes.) A short descent down a steep gully leads to the slow, shallow waters of the Wollangambe.

7 A wide stretch of sand on the opposite bank offers a perfect picnic spot and an idyllic spot to while away the hours. A rough track leads upstream for 200 metres to the junction of Bell Creek and Wollangambe, and from here you can wade upstream into a tall ravine on your right. Alternatively, you can wade downstream for a distance, until the water gets too deep or you're ready to return the way you came.

The scribbly gum referred to in waymark 4

Fire trail at Mount Wilson

Canyoning in the Blue Mountains

Canyoning can be a truly sublime outdoor experience. Imagine secret ravines, clear deep pools, narrow chasms, hidden cascades and floating on a lilo downstream between towering rock walls. The Blue Mountains offers some of the best canyoning in the world, and the upper sections of the Wollangambe are very popular, as they are relatively easy to access and don't involve abseiling. However, even the simplest of canyons requires proper equipment, including thermals, dry bags, wetsuits and lilos. On the Wollangambe, the water is both deep and extremely cold, and the combination of fatigue and chill can be profound. Unless you've been canyoning before, you're best to go on an organised trip the first few times (try out High n Wild at www.high-n-wild.com.au or Blue Mountains Adventure Company at www.bmac.com.au).

Jenolan Caves boasts 11 magnificent world-class caves, with more than three kilometres of underground paths, all strategically lit to display a maze of ancient limestone caverns and subterranean rivers. This bushwalk explores the area immediately in the vicinity of the caves, circling up to Carlotta Arch, through the Devils Coachhouse, circuiting the Blue Lake and returning through the Grand Arch.

Finding the track

The track starts opposite the foyer of Caves House, clearly signposted to Carlotta Arch.

At a glance

Grade: Easy (but many steps)

Time: 1 hour (allow extra for Nettle Cave)

Distance: 2 km circuit

Ascent/Descent: 110 metres descent, 110 metres ascent

Weather: All conditions

Closest public transport: Bus from Katoomba leaves 9.45am daily. T 4782 7999

Looking through Carlotta Arch to Blue Lake

Walk 66 Natural wonders at Jenolan Caves

Walk directions

1 Follow the gentle grade uphill. Looking across to your right is the body of mountain under which most of Jenolan's caves lie.

2 As you come across the rise of the hill, you can see the Blue Lake below, framed by Carlotta Arch, the remains of an old cave that eroded away millions of years ago. (Steps descend through the Arch, but come to a dead-end half way.) Continue along the main path.

3 The Six Foot Track branches off to the right, but go a little further and take the next path on your right, signposted to the Devils Coach House. (Just beyond this intersection is an enormous hole on the left-hand side, called the Plug Hole, where abseilers enter to explore the Elder Cave.) Halfway down, explore the little sidetrack to the right which takes you to the 'Peephole', with views down to the Devils Coach House below.

4 At a T-junction on McKeowns Creek, head right. You're now walking through the Devils Coach House, a cavernous natural archway named after a nervous camper who swore he saw the devil himself storming through the cave aboard a horse-drawn coach. Way above, the roof arch reaches 57 metres at its highest point.

5 If you have purchased tickets to view any of the other caves at Jenolan, you can swipe the barcode on your free Jenolan Pass to access the naturally-lit Nettle Cave (accessed from within the Coach House), which features stalactites, stalagmites and many other ancient formations. After the bustle of viewing caves with a tour group, exploring this cave at your own pace is a real pleasure.

6 As you emerge from the Coach House, cross the road and follow signs for the River Walk. The Blue Lake gets its deep-blue

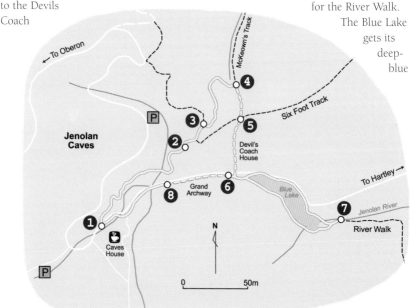

Temple of Baal Cave

colour from light refracting through clay particles in the water. If you come here at dawn or dusk, you may be lucky enough to spot a platypus.

7 Beyond the lake, a metal bridge takes you down to a set of cascades with a small pool below (a much safer swimming spot that the weir at the Blue Lake). From here, you can continue along the river as far as you have the energy (points of interest further on include a rickety suspension bridge and the hydro-electric power station at the end, but the weeds are a problem along the river banks, detracting from

Suspension bridge over Jenolan River

the area's natural beauty). When you return, cross the river on the metal bridge just beyond the weir to circle back on the northern side.

8 Return to Caves House by following the road through the Grand Arch.

Katoomba, Leura

KATOOMBA

LEURA

Katoomba

Leura

Blue Mountains National Park

Jamison Valley

Three Sisters

Scenic World

Leura Cascades

Katoomba Falls

N

0   1km

& Wentworth Falls

To
18, 32
& 34

Blue
Mountains
National
Park

Hay
Rd

Blaxland

Rd

Wentworth
Falls
Lake

Great

Scott Ave

Western

Wentworth
Falls

Rd

WENTWORTH
FALLS

39
43

Gladstone
Rd

St

Fitzroy St

Valley

Rd

Conservation
Hut

41

Fletcher

Falls

St

Creek

Highway

31 33
46

37 40
42 44
45 47

Sublime Point Rd

Blue
Mountains
National
Park

Jamison

Great   Western

Highway

Railway   Leura

LEURA

Pde

Leura Mall

Grose   St

Wascoe St

Quinns Ave

Megalong   St

Rd

Queen
Elizabeth Dr
38

Tableland

WENTWORTH FALLS (inset)

Matcham Ave

Adele Ave

Great

Western

Cascade St

Falls Rd

Plantation St

Station St

Railway Pde

Wentworth
Falls

Ave

Wilson
Park

WENTWORTH
FALLS

Highway

Taylor

Dalrymple Ave

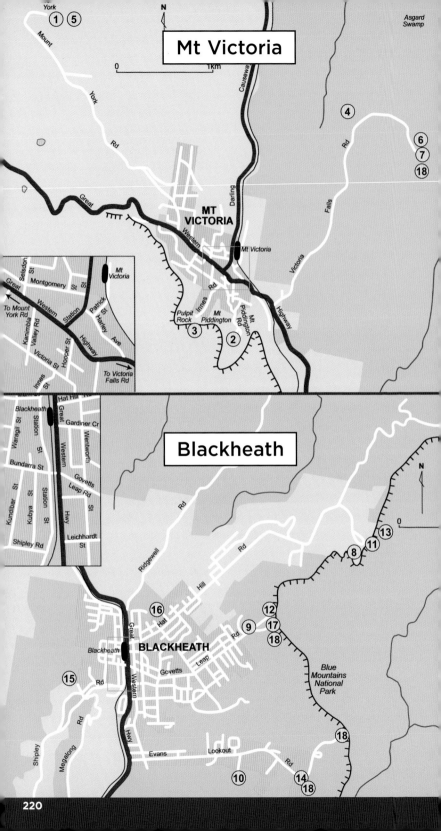

Mt Victoria

Blackheath

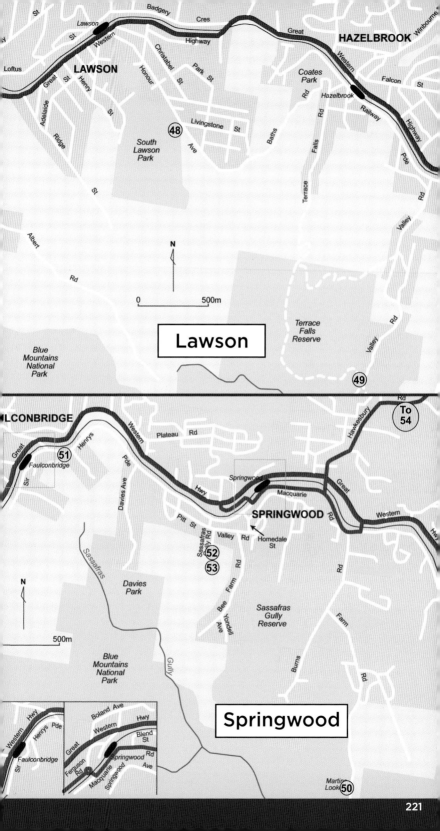

Lawson

LAWSON

HAZELBROOK

Badgery Cres

Lawson St

Western

Great

Great

Western

Railway

Highway

Loftus

Adelaide

Ridge

Great

St

Henry

St

Honour

Christabel

Park St

St

Coates Park

Falcon St

Hazelbrook

Christabel

Livingstone St

South Lawson Park

Baths

Falls

Rd

Rd

Pde

Hazelbrook Railway

Highway

Valley

Albert

Rd

Terrace

Valley

Rd

St

Rd

㊽

N

0   500m

Lawson

Blue Mountains National Park

Terrace Falls Reserve

㊾

Springwood

FALCONBRIDGE

SPRINGWOOD

Great

Western

Plateau   Rd

Rd

Hawkesbury

Rd

To 54

Faulconbridge

Henrys

Pde

Sir

�51

Davies Ave

Springwood

Hwy

Macquarie

Great

Rd

Western

Hwy

Pitt   St

Valley   Rd

Homedale St

Sassafras

Sassafras Gully Rd

�52

�53

Rd

N

Davies Park

Bee Farm Ave

Yondell

Sassafras Gully Reserve

Farm   Rd

500m

Gully

Blue Mountains National Park

Burns

Rd

Springwood

Western   Hwy

Henrys Pde

Boland Ave

Hwy

Western

Blend St

Faulconbridge

Sir

Great

Ferguson Rd

Macquarie

Springwood   Rd

Ave

Martins Lookout

㊿

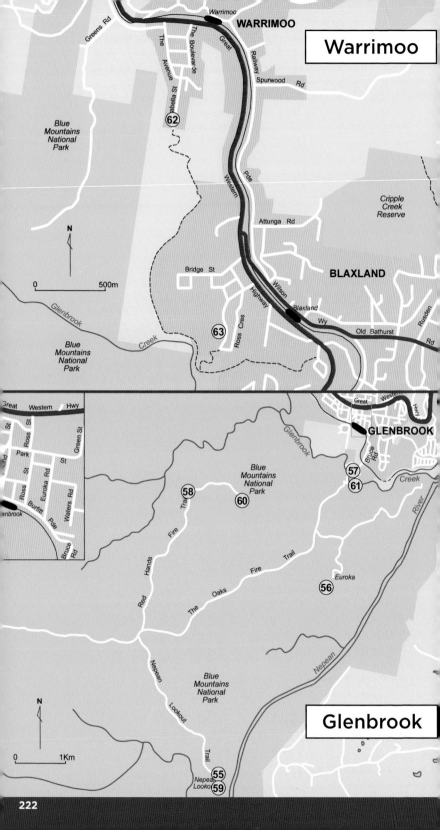

Guided Walks

If you're not in the Blue Mountains for long then joining up with a club may not be the way to go. However, guided walks by tour companies are a great way to learn about the bush and get a deeper appreciation of the Blue Mountains environment. You also have the opportunity to do trips that are just that bit more adventurous than what you'd be prepared to take on if you went by yourself.

- **Tread Lightly eco tours** is run by Tim Tranter, one of the most respected interpretative guides in the Blue Mountains. Walking tours emphasise the educational and sensory experiences of being in the bush. Tread Lightly is fully licensed with NPWS and has advanced ecotourism accreditation. **www.treadlightly.com.au T 4788 1229**.

- **Blue Mountains Walkabout** run educational tours with an emphasis on the Aboriginal cultural features of the Blue Mountains, Owned and operated by Aboriginal guides, the tour follows a traditional walkabout song line. **www.bluemountainswalkabout.com T 0408 443 822**.

- The well-established and reputable **High n Wild** offer all the regular abseiling/climbing trips, but also offer interpretative guided walks including bush tucker walks, bush medicine walks, navigation courses, and bush skill survival courses. **www.high-n-wild.com.au T 4782 6224**.

- The **National Parks and Wildlife Service** run a series of walks, talks and tours called the Discovery program. Developed and led by a group of local rangers, the idea of this program is to share knowledge about the Blue Mountains environment and the history that created it. Although the dates and choice of walks aren't as flexible as a private company, rates are very affordable. **www.npws.nsw.gov.au T 4787 8877**.

- **Blue Mountain Guides** run photo safaris, half-day and full-day walks, wilderness expeditions and wildflower walks. **www.bluemountainsguides.com.au T 4782 6109**.

Bushwalking Clubs

If you're looking for a bit of companionship while you're out there communing in the bush, why not join a bushwalking club?

- The **Confederation of Bushwalking Clubs NSW** is a confederation of individual Bushwalking Clubs that represents the interests of member bushwalking clubs. Visit **www.bushwalking.org.au** to follow links to bushwalking clubs throughout NSW.

- The **Blue Mountains Conservation Society** is a local conservation group that also runs regular weekly walks of all kinds. Information regarding membership and walk timetables is available from **www.bluemountains.org.au** or by contacting the walks convenor. **T 4757 1872**.

- **The Bush Club** was established in 1939 by Marie Byles and Paddy Pallin. The club runs a variety of graded walks, including walks to more remote areas taking two or more days. **www.bushclub.org.au T 9144 2096**.

- The **National Parks Association of NSW** has the largest activities program of its kind in Australia, offering around 800 walks per year, led by over 200 experienced volunteer walks leaders. There's a whole range of walks, from easy excursion through to full pack overnight treks, NPA caters for every ability and interest. **www.npansw.org.au**. **T 9299 0000**

- The **Upper Blue Mountains Bushwalking Club i**s based in the Upper Blue Mountains and has been active for over 20 years. **T 4787 7432** or **visit www.ubmbc.org.au**

Index

Index

Index

Index

Map Symbols and Legend

🖼	Aboriginal site	≪	View Point/Lookout
🍖	BBQ	❶ ○	Waypoint
▭	Bridge	⊥⊥⊥⊥	Escarpment/Cliff
🚌	Bus Stop		Fire Trail
☕	Café	▬▬▬	Highway
△	Camping Area	☁	Lake/Large River
🎢	Childrens Playground		River/Creek
⋈	Locked Gate	▬●▬	Railway Station
🅿	Parking		Road
•	Point of Interest	═══	Walking Route
🪑	Seating bench	-------	Walking Track
🎍	Picnic table		
T	Toilet		
ⓘ	Tourist information	0 200m	Scale

N

About the author

Veechi Stuart is a freelance author, journalist and former Sydney Morning Herald columnist. Veechi has lived in the Blue Mountains since 1987 and is passionate about bushwalking, the local community and the environment. Veechi is also the author of *Sydney's Best Bush, Park & City Walks* and co-author of *Sydney's Best Picnic Spots, Parks and Reserves*.

Acknowledgments

The author acknowledges and thanks the Darug and Gundungarra people, original custodians of the Blue Mountains.

Also, thanks to everyone at Woodslane who helped to get this book off the ground, in particular Andrew Swaffer, Dave Scott, Katrina O'Brien and Coral Lee. Thank you to Scott Townsend for his beautiful and inspiring photographs.

Thanks also to those who were so generous with their professional advice and assistance: Wayne Brennan (Burramoko Archaeological Services), Dave Crestani (Mt Tomah Botanic Gardens), Lachlan Garland (fellow bushwalker), Aine Gliddon, Christopher Woods, Louise Sheehan (National Parks and Wildlife), Michael Bull (Bull Artistry), Karen McLaughlin and Andrew Valja (our meticulous cartographers), Tony Fakira and Erica McIntyre (additional cartography), Amy St Lawrence (Streamwatch, Blue Mountains City Council), Chris Tobin (Darug community) John Merriman

(local historian) and Tim Tranter (Tread Lightly eco tours). Also, thank you to Jim Smith, whose guides to walking in the Blue Mountains inspired a generation of bushwalkers and kept many forgotten tracks alive.

Photography

Most of the photographs in this book were taken by Scott Townsend, with additional photography by the author, Veechi Curtis. Additional photography has been supplied by Scenic World, Simon Barrett, Robbie Begg, Romain Cailliau, Jenolan Caves Trust, Lithgow Tourism, John Merriman, Julian Robinson, Finbar Stuart and John Stuart.

Photo front cover (The Three Sisters), Timapatt Talalak. Photo front cover (greater glider), Julian Robinson. Page 17, John Stuart. Page 21, John Stuart. Pages 37 and 47, John Merriman. Page 65, Simon Barrett. Page 71, John Merriman. Page 83, Scenic World. Page 206 and page 217, Jenolan Caves Trust. Page 203 and page 205 (top), John Stuart. Page 210 (bottom), Romain Cailliau. Page 211, Lithgow Tourism Authority. Page 212 and 214, Robbie Begg. Page 215, Finbar Stuart.

Woodslane Press

Blue Mountains Best Bushwalks is just one of a growing series of outdoor guides from Sydney publishers Woodslane Press. To browse through other titles available from Woodslane Press, visit www.woodslane.com.au. If your local bookshop does not have stock of a Woodslane Press book, they can easily order it for you. In case of difficulty please contact our customer service team on 02 9970 5111 or or see www.outdoorbooks.com.au.

Titles include:

Sydney's Best Bush, Park & City Walks 2/e

After sharing the delights of the *Blue Mountains Best Bushwalks*, author Veechi Stuart turns her attention to the wealth of bush, park and city walks to be found in and around Sydney. With all the major local National Parks included and many otherwise rarely visited tracks given a new lease of life, *Sydney's Best Bush, Park & City Walks* will enthuse even the most experienced walkers. *Sydney's Best Bush, Park & City Walks* completes this series of walking guides to the near-Sydney region.

$29.95 • ISBN: 9781921203145

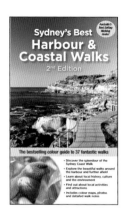

Sydney's Best Harbour & Coastal Walks 2/e

From Barrenjoey Head to the Royal National Park, Hen & Chicken Bay to North and South Heads, local author Katrina O'Brien takes us on an enriching tour of over 35 of the very best walks to be experienced along the shores of Sydney's harbour and coast. Like all our guides, the book includes full colour photography and maps, easy-to-follow instructions and great local information. *Sydney's Best Harbour & Coastal Walks* will be a treasured companion.

$29.95 • ISBN: 9781921874468

Sydney's Best Picnic Spots, Parks & Reserves

$29.95 • ISBN: 9781921203879

Sydney's Best Beaches & Rock Baths

$29.95 • ISBN: 9781921203367

Sydney's Best Dog-friendly Walks, Parks & Places to Play

$29.95 • ISBN: 9781921683855

4WD Treks Close To Sydney

$39.95 • ISBN: 9781921606137

Camping Guide to New South Wales and the ACT 5/e

$29.95 • ISBN: 9781921203688

Surfing New South Wales

$34.95 • ISBN: 9781921606007

Your thoughts appreciated!

We do hope that you are enjoying using this book, but we know that nothing in this world is perfect and your suggestions for improving on this edition would be much appreciated.

Your name _____   _____

Your address or email address _____

_____

_____

Your contact phone number   _____

Are you a resident or visitor to Blue Mountains? _____

What you most liked about this book _____

_____

_____

What you least liked about this book _____

_____

_____

Which is your favourite walk featured in this book?

_____

Which walk wasn't featured but you think should have been included?

_____

Would you like us to keep you informed of other Woodslane books?

If so: are you interested in:

- ☐ walking
- ☐ visiting natural & historic sites
- ☐ picnicking
- ☐ cycling
- ☐ general outdoor activities
- ☐ activities in the Sydney region only
- ☐ activities in NSW
- ☐ activities around Australia

What others books would you like to see in this series?

_____

_____

_____

Woodslane Pty Ltd • 7/5 Vuko Place • Warriewood • NSW 2102
Fax: 02 9970 5002 • Email: walks@woodslane.com.au